CONTENTS

INTRODUCTION | 6

CHAPTER 1
DIET AND NUTRITION | 7

CHAPTER 2
MUSCLE STARTS IN THE KITCHEN | 14

CHAPTER 3
EATING TO BUILD MUSCLE | 17

CHAPTER 4
EATING TO BURN FAT & GET SHREDDED | 22

CHAPTER 5
PRE & POST WORKOUT NUTRITION | 25

CHAPTER 6
BREAKFAST | 28

Mighty Quinoa Breakfast Cereal | 29
Bounty Oats | 30
Brawny Buckwheat Breakfast | 31
Sizzling Sausage Patties | 32
Get-Fit Frittata | 33
Eggs In Avocados! | 34
Brilliant Breakfast Bircher | 35
Mighty Meatloaves | 36
Score-Board Scotch Eggs | 37
Epic Egg Muffins | 38
Turkey Bacon Omelette | 39
Banana & Hazelnut Oatmeal || 40
Perfect Pancakes | 41
Workout Waffles | 42
Strengthening Spinach Scramble | 43
Sweet Potato Pancakes | 44
Classic Steak, Mushroom & Eggs | 45
Pumpin' Pumpkin Pancakes | 46
Bodybuilder's Banana Pancakes | 47
Cherry Protein Porridge | 48

CHAPTER 7
POULTRY | 49

Artichoke & Tomato Chicken Bake | 50
Cajun Chicken | 51
Chicken Burgers & Guacamole | 52
Divine Duck Breasts | 53
Tasty Turkey Burgers | 54
Oven-Baked Chicken Thighs | 55
Nourishing Nutty Noodles | 56
Training Turkey Kebabs | 57
Carrot Noodles & Cilantro Chicken | 58
Powerful Pesto Chicken | 59
Mediterranean Chicken & Eggplant | 60
Bodybuilding Fajitas | 61
Mighty Stuffed Peppers | 62

Caribbean Turkey Thighs | 63
Chicken With Homemade Slaw | 64
Cheeky Chicken Curry | 65
Lemon Chicken With Swede & Kale Puree | 66
Tomato, Mozzarella & Basil Chicken | 67
Turkey & Cranberry Sauce | 68
Tandoori Style Chicken Drumsticks | 69
Turkey Meatballs & Couscous | 70

CHAPTER 8

MEAT | 71

Roasted Rump & Root Veg | 72
Mix 'N' Match Beef Burger | 73
Fit Lamb Steaks With Tzatziki | 74
Bodybuilding Beef Stew | 75
Muscle Meatball & Celeriac Spaghetti | 76
Lemongrass & Chili Beef | 77
Powerful Pork & Speedy Sauerkraut | 78
Muscle-Friendly Lasagne | 79
Barbell Beef Curry | 80
Chili Beef & Mango Salsa | 81
Chunky Chinese Stir Fry | 82
Moroccan Lamb Tagine | 83
Lean Beef Stroganoff | 84
Chili Beef In Lettuce Tortillas | 85
Beef & Pearl Barley Casserole | 86
Eggplant & Sweet Potato Lasagne | 87
Steak, Egg & Mushroom Frenzy | 88
Red Thai Curry With Duck | 89
Slow Cooked Spicy Steak & Beans | 90
Sweet Potato Cottage Pie | 91
Beef Chili Con Carne | 92

CHAPTER 9

VEGETARIAN & VEGAN | 93

Training Tofu Broth | 94
Mexican Beans & Quinoa | 95
Vegan Lasagne 96
Toasted Sesame & Peanut Tofu | 97

Halloumi Burgers & Chili Ketchup | 98
Strong Spaghetti Squash Quinoa | 99
Spiced Cauliflower & Chickpea Curry | 100
Garlic Stuffed Mushrooms | 101
Creamy Walnut Penne | 102
Pumpkin & Pine Nut Casserole | 103
Chinese Tempah Stir Fry | 104
Aesthetic Asparagus & Beetroot Tart | 105
Raisin & Root Veg Stew | 106
Spanish Paella | 107
Kino Kedgeree | 108
Zesty Zucchini Pasta & Protein Peas | 109
Scallion & Goats Cheese Pancakes | 110
Chili & Honey Squash With Crispy Kale & Tofu | 111
Lime & Ginger Tempah | 112

CHAPTER 10

SEAFOOD | 113

Calamari & Shrimp Paella | 114
Salmon Fillet & Pesto Mash | 115
Fennel & Olive Sea Bass | 116
Bulk-Up Sardines With Lemon, Garlic & Parsley | 117
Cod, Pea & Spinach Risotto | 118
Rainbow Trout | 119
Langoustine & Sweet Potato Fries | 120
Tomato & Walnut Sole | 121
Salmon Burgers With Avocado | 122
Heavy Haddock & Bean Stew | 123
Asian Spiced Halibut | 124
Terrific Tuna Nicoise | 125
Sesame Monkfish & Fruit Salsa | 126
Ginger & Honey Mahi-Mahi With Orange Salad | 127
Smoked Trout Fish Cakes | 128
Scallops With Cauliflower & Chili | 129
Coconut Shrimp & Noodles | 130
Spicy Swordfish Steaks | 131
Thai Training Broth | 132
Garlic & Lemon Shrimp Linguine | 133
Mighty Mussel Broth | 134
Tuna Steaks With Nutty Green Beans | 135
Chunky Cod Parcels | 136
Haddock & Kale Crumble | 137
Seafood Kebabs & Cucumber Salad | 138

THE ESSENTIAL

BODYBUILDING COOKBOOK

150 | HEALTHY, SIMPLE & DELICIOUS BODYBUILDING RECIPES TO MEET YOUR EVERY NEED

RYAN POWELL

CP

CARRILLO PRESS

ISBN-13: 978-1911364078
ISBN-10: 1911364073

CHAPTER 11

SOUPS | 139

Carrot, Quinoa & Tarragon Soup | 140
Spaghetti Squash & Yellow Lentil Soup | 141
Red Pepper & Pinto Bean Soup | 142
Chicken & Lemongrass Soup | 143
Curried Chickpea & Garlic Soup | 144
Nutmeg, Spinach & Pork Soup | 145
White Bean & Med Veg Soup | 146
Healthy Vegetable Stock | 147
Lean Chicken Stock | 148

CHAPTER 12

SIDES, SALADS & SNACKS | 149

Pear & Pecan Chips | 150
Mixed Seed Topper | 151
Blueberry Energy Burst | 152
Parsnip & Rutabaga Chips | 153
Homemade Sweet Potato Fries | 154
Red Pepper Hummus | 155
Powerful Pumpkin Mash | 156
Latin Rice | 157
Nutty Green Beans & Broccoli | 158
Turkey & Tabbouleh Salad | 159
Spinach Pesto & Crudities | 160
Goats' Cheese, Endive & Pomegranate Salad | 161
Cucumber, Poppy Seed & Arugula Salad | 162
Zucchini, Bulghar Wheat And Eggplant Salad | 163
Butter Bean, Tomato & Spring Onion Salad | 164
Crab & Arugula Salad | 165

CHAPTER 13

SHAKES, DRINKS & DESSERTS | 166

Chocolate & Berry Shake | 167
Brilliant Banana Shake | 168
Tangerine Twist | 169
Power Protein Shake | 170
Immune Boost | 171
Lemon Boost | 172
Ginger & Lemon Green Iced-Tea | 173
Banana & Peanut Milkshake | 174
Yogurt Shake | 175
Crunchy Apple Pie | 176
Strawberry Mousse | 177
Pecan & Dark Chocolate Chip Cookies | 178
Raspberry & Vanilla Muffins | 179
Raisin & Coconut Boosters | 180
Vanilla Pancakes & Apricots | 181

APPENDIX

CONVERSION TABLES | 182
REFERENCES | 184
INDEX | 185

INTRODUCTION

Thank you for buying The Essential Bodybuilding Cookbook. So, your bodybuilding and training is very important to you and you want to eat well. It may be that you are just starting out, or you're a pro, but either way you're looking for a variety of meals to help you gain muscle and shift fat.

You've come to the right place!

This cookbook contains 150 recipes dedicated to the body builder; choose from breakfasts, meat, poultry, seafood, vegetarian, sides, salads, snacks, soups and even healthy protein shakes and desserts. Each of the recipes has been created using healthy, fresh and easy to come by ingredients. More importantly, they're all delicious and there's no way you're going to get bored. Not only that, but these meals need not only be enjoyed by you alone - they can be prepared for a loved one or even the whole family.

As well as the recipes, I have also provided chapters on the best food and nutrition as well as specific formulae for calculating your daily intake of food, specific to you and your training needs. So whether you're looking to bulk up or shred down - we've got it covered.

Use the food and kitchen lists to stock up your kitchen and the sample meal plans as an idea of how you could space your meals over the day. I've also included information about all the macronutrients - protein, fats and carbohydrates and given examples of the 'good' foods that fall under each category.

With your motivation, all this information, and one of the biggest collections of body building recipes out there, I'm sure that you are going to succeed in your training goals!

100% Training + 100% Nutrition + 100% Rest = 100% RESULTS

Enjoy!

1
DIET AND NUTRITION

When we start on our bodybuilding journey, we must remember that it doesn't matter how strict you are with your training regime, how many reps you can do, or how heavy you can lift - if you are not eating a healthy, balanced diet with the right amount of protein, fats and carbohydrates, then all of your hard work at the gym will be in vain.

Unfortunately, most people sign up for a gym membership and go ahead and pump away, without understanding the need for proper nutrition. More often than not, they spend a lot of time, energy, and money before winding up with zero results and blaming it on external factors such as genetics, poor equipment, and even poor personal trainers!

A common misconception about bodybuilding is that all fuel is good fuel. People may think that it's all about the calorie intake - they've got to eat as much as possible to bulk up and turn it into muscle -but it isn't quite as easy as that.

Energy is used for everything we do in life – walking, working, running, talking, and yes, bodybuilding. But you also need energy for things that we sometimes take for granted. When you sleep, you still breath, your blood still pumps as your heart works, and you still expend energy. To expend energy, human beings need fuel. Think of an automobile needing gasoline to run. Without gasoline, it won't start, much less drive anywhere. Your body works in the same way, but unlike cars that don't use up energy when they're in the garage overnight, your body uses up tons of energy while you're sleeping!

If you want to get the ultimate body, the fuel that you put into it needs to be just right. This is why nutrition is so important. As previously mentioned, sometimes people can actually wind up sabotaging their own training plans exactly because they don't know what to eat. Moreover, the things they do eat, instead of helping them build muscle mass, cause them to lose muscle, weight and energy. There goes the bodybuilding goals! Keep reading to learn more about the diet and what is important to consider.

CALORIES

Each calorie is a unit of energy. If you don't consume enough calories, the activity in your brain actually slows down and you lose energy. If you consume too many calories, this will lead to weight gain and the many health problems related to that condition.

It is important therefore to know how many calories you should be eating, taking into consideration your gender, exercise regime and body building goals. Frayn's text on metabolic regulation lists the following formula:

Energy intake (food) = Energy expended (heat + work) + Energy stored

Look at it this way: it's the beginning of your training day, and you eat a balanced breakfast, which means that you'll be eating a specific number of calories. When these calories enter your body, the following things can happen to them:

- Some will be stored as fat (meaning energy you can use in the future),
- Some will be transferred into your body's cells to be converted into the energy that you need to get through your exercises,
- Some will be immediately converted into heat.

The challenge is to make sure that you know how many calories you'll need to eat, and where you'll be getting those calories from: some must be used immediately so you can jump right into your workout; some must be stored for use over the rest of the day; and some must be used so that your body itself can keep going.

The level of your energy balance is the balance between the calories you consume and those that you burn through physical activity. What you eat is INCOMING ENERGY, and what you burn up through physical activity is OUTGOING

ENERGY.

Energy Balance = Energy Intake - Energy Expenditure

So -

If ENERGY IN (calories eaten) and ENERGY OUT (calories burned) are the same over time = your weight stays the same.

If ENERGY IN (calories eaten) are less than ENERGY OUT (calories burned) over time = you will lose weight. This is also called NEGATIVE ENERGY BALANCE.

If ENERGY IN (calories eaten) are more than ENERGY OUT (calories burned) over time = your weight will increase. This is also called POSITIVE ENERGY BALANCE.

To further help you understand what your food is made up of and what you need to be consuming you need to know about macronutrients (the nutrients we need for cell growth, cell repair, energy usage and to maintain bodily functions). There are three basic sources of fuel that provide energy:

PROTEIN

Protein molecules are the building blocks for muscle; the object of our bodybuilding efforts. All of the cells in your body contain protein. Protein is made up of amino acids and is used to resupply, rebuild, and repair muscle cells and also perform a wide range of other functions in your body, including the replication of DNA, transporting molecules, responding to stimuli, and catalyzing metabolic reactions. Over 2/3 of protein in your body resides in your muscles.

Proteins come in a variety of forms including animal sources (meats, dairy products, fish, and eggs) as well as plant sources including nuts (almonds, cashew nuts, walnuts), legumes (peas, beans, lentils) and grains (corn, wheat, oats). Most people will consume the recommended amount of protein by eating a balanced diet. Depending on your goals though, it might be necessary to increase your intake of protein using supplements such as protein powders.

CARBOHYDRATES

Carbohydrates are used by the body as the first and most accessible source of energy. Again, they come in many forms (some better for us than others) and include the following amongst others:

- Grains (rice and wheat)
- Fruits (most contain fructose)
- Milk
- Vegetables
- Table sugar, and Splenda (sucrose)
- Candy and syrup
- Beans and legumes

When carbohydrates are ingested, they are converted into blood glucose through the process of glycolysis, before being absorbed through the small intestines and then entering the bloodstream; this causes blood glucose levels to rise. This process of making and transporting glucose triggers a very important hormonal action - the pancreas makes insulin, a peptide that helps take the sugar to the cells so that they can use it as energy. This metabolic process is essential but can go wrong when we eat too many carbohydrates or sugars.

When there is too much glucose in the bloodstream, the pancreas secretes more insulin. This moves excess glucose in the blood to other tissues, for instance the muscles, to be stored in the form of glycogen. Excess glycogen is then pushed into fat cells for storage. If there's enough glucose in the body, it is the preferred fuel for most tissues, but any excess amount is embedded into muscle tissue, leading to excess fat stores. Carbohydrate fuel needs constant re-supply to give the human body a feeling of being satiated or "full."

Carbohydrates are the human body's key source of energy. Without glucose, both the body and the brain itself would slow down and become impaired. However, it is the processed carbohydrates that we need to watch out for as these have led to a variety of illnesses prevalent today.

THE GLYCEMIC INDEX

GI measures the extent to which a food carbohydrate can be classified as simple or complex. This classification is based on the food's chemical composition as well as how quickly the sugars in the food are synthesized and absorbed in your body. The GI measures how a given food product affects the blood sugar levels; it measures the relative rise in the raise of blood sugar levels following the consumption of that food product. Simple carbohydrates break down more easily during the process of digestion, which means that high levels of glucose enter the body in a short period of time. These products e.g. white bread, white rice, cornflakes, certain processed breakfast cereals and peeled white potatoes, tend to have high glycemic indexes.

The opposite is true for food products made with complex carbohydrates: it takes a longer time for these to be broken down by the body, resulting in a gradual and more controlled release of glucose into the blood. These products tend to have low glycemic indexes: beans, fruits and vegetables, and mushrooms fall into this category.

In the long term, and in the context of your bodybuilding goals, consuming low-GI foods is more beneficial: what you get is a controlled release of energy over a longer period of time, which means you can do more, lift more, and come out on top in terms of your health.

FATS

Although this sounds like a taboo word in the bodybuilding world, or for anyone looking to get fit for that matter, the human body actually needs certain kinds of fats in order to survive. We store energy in the form of fat so that it can be used as energy.

We do however, need to be aware of the different types of fats: saturated, trans fats and unsaturated. It's been claimed by many health organizations from all over the world that the high intake of saturated fats might be to blame for conditions like cardiovascular disease, diabetes, and certain forms of cancer. Saturated fats are those found in fattier cuts of meat, butter, milk, lard and those in pies, cookies and baked products. You can switch to leaner cuts of meat instead of fatty ones, from full-fat milk to non-fat milk and cut out baked and packaged products as much as possible.

Trans fats are artificial fats, created by a process in the factory. They are found in foods such as packaged foods, margarines, some frying oils and fast foods. Trans fats, increase cholesterol and should be avoided as much as possible.

Unsaturated fats are the fats you should be eating. These are commonly known as 'healthy fats' and are vital to a healthy diet. They include omega-3 and omega-6 fatty acids which are found in fish, shellfish, olive oil, and leafy vegetables.

WATER

Hydration is critical. The human body is composed of at least 60% water and it is contained in literally every cell, every organ, and every system in the human body. It is important to drink lots of water before and during your workouts because water makes it easier for the heart to pump blood and nutrients through the body. Water also helps muscles to move more efficiently.

You might now be wondering about the effectiveness of products like energy drinks and sports drinks, and while they can be useful in providing the electrolytes that you lose during your workouts, these kinds of drinks can be loaded with extra sugars or large amounts of sodium. Use sparingly and not as a replacement for water.

ALCOHOL

Alcohol is a diuretic - it forces your kidneys to do much more work to break it down. This means you will produce more urine and in turn become dehydrated.

Being dehydrated means your muscles grow weaker and you can't tap into your body's energy reserves as efficiently as you normally would. Alcohol has other negative effects on your body: it can actually cause you to lose muscle tissue, because the alcohol disrupts the process of creating and maintaining muscle cells. It's your decision whether you're going to give up alcohol whilst training or not but there is no two ways about it - it will impair the process. I believe moderation is the key.

2
MUSCLE STARTS IN THE KITCHEN

The following are four principles for stocking your kitchen:

PRINCIPLE 1: Whole, fresh foods are better than packaged or processed. Avoid foods with added sugar, salt, fat and preservatives. Switch to cooking methods that don't add salt or fat.

PRINCIPLE 2: Pre-planning is essential. Plan the meals and snacks you will need for the week ahead. Buy as much as you can fresh and freeze what will go off before the end of the week - just remember to take it out 24 hours before cooking to defrost. Fish out or purchase a set of Tupperware boxes that can be used in the microwave. You'll need about 10 containers for meals. Small containers for snacks are a bonus! You'll also benefit from purchasing zip-up sandwich bags, baking paper and/or cooking foil.

PRINCIPLE 3: Buying whole, fresh foods can be more expensive but be savvy and choose markets/grocery stores with better deals and stick to what you need after you've planned to avoid waste.

PRINCIPLE 4: Remove temptations, Look in your kitchen and pantry for processed foods and take them out right now! This includes the following:

- Processed baked goods, including doughnuts,
- Candy,
- Deli meats, such as bacon, pastrami, and ham,
- Potato chips and similar snack food items,
- Fruit juices with added sugar,
- Sugary breakfast cereals.

YOUR GROCERY LIST

Low GI Carbs:

- Whole-wheat bread and pasta,
- Rolled or steel-cut oats -- not the quick-cooking or instant stuff,
- Brown rice,
- Quinoa,
- Sweet potatoes.

Proteins:

- Eggs and egg whites,
- Fatty fish, such as salmon, tuna and sardines,
- Lean fish, such as tilapia, mahi mahi,
- Beef - where possible, choose loin or round cuts,
- Skinless chicken and turkey breasts,
- Lean ground meats (beef, turkey, pork)
- Canned fish - packed in water and not oil,
- Beans -- kidney beans, pinto beans, lima beans etc.,
- Tofu.

Good fats:

- Milk (skimmed),
- Cottage cheese,
- Greek yogurt,
- Olive oil,
- Coconut oil,
- Avocado,
- Whole peanut butter,
- Nuts and seeds.

All fruit and vegetables: Remember to buy your fruits and vegetables when they're in season for maximum taste and optimal nutrition. Alternatively frozen varieties are just as healthy.

Herbs and spices: Choose chili flakes, thyme, oregano, paprika etc. to add flavor to your meals and stop you reaching for the salt.

COOKING AND MEAL PREP ESSENTIALS

1. Baking, boiling, steaming or broiling is better than frying. If frying, use olive oil or coconut oil instead of sunflower or vegetable oils. Olive oil cooking sprays are also great for controlling the amount you use.

2. Set aside one day a week to prepare meals in advance and portion up into containers so that they're ready to go!

3. Cook in bulk and portion up meals. Meat can be kept in the fridge for 2-3 days as well as the carbohydrates and vegetables you prepare. Keep the rest in the freezer and defrost 24 hours in advance of eating. Alternatively prep meals 2 days a week for the following 2-3 days.

4. Know how many meals/snacks you will eat per day in order to prepare.

3
EATING TO BUILD MUSCLE

Let's get this out of the way – going on a diet doesn't mean you are not allowed to eat tasty food. You can, and when you are bulking up, you will be doing a hell of a lot of eating. In lean muscle building, it simply means being mindful of what you eat.

The principle of eating to build muscle is quite similar to eating to lose weight: you need to compute your calorie intake. You need to know how many calories you need to consume in order to successfully build your muscle.

WHY YOU CAN'T GAIN WEIGHT

There is only one major reason behind the lack of weight gain – calorie deficit. Your intake of calories should be greater than the calories you use up.

If you're skinny and you're gunning for gains, it can be frustrating to force yourself to eat, hoping to get bigger. If you're taking in enough calories, then you should gain at least a few pounds, right?

The most obvious factor behind calorie deficit is that you're not eating enough food consistently. You should eat regularly with each meal consisting of quality protein, unsaturated fats, and complex carbs.

HOW MANY CALORIES DO YOU NEED FOR EXTREME MUSCLE GROWTH?

The most important concept in calorie intake is determining what your calorie maintenance level (CML) is. That level is the approximate amount of calorie intake that you need to maintain your weight if you were to eat without exercising. A rough calculation is done by multiplying your current body weight by 15. For example, if you are 200 pounds, your CML will be 3,000 calories per day. Eating 3,000 calories per day will leave you at your current 200-pound level.

If you want to gain muscle, you will need to eat around 10% over your CML or in this example about 300 calories (3,000 x 10%). Now you have to make sure that you eat at least 3,300 calories per day.

You need to weigh yourself at a selected "starting point" in the week. This should be a morning when you have not yet taken in any food or water. A good starting day would be a Monday morning. You need to monitor what happens to your weight on a weekly basis, and depending on your objectives, you should see the following results if you are counting your calories correctly:

With the objective to gain muscle or increase strength, you should be aiming to gain 2 pounds per month. If you are gaining less than ½ pound a week, or are not gaining any weight at all, you need to increase your calorie intake by another 10%. In the case of the 3,000 calorie per day, 200 pound man, this means increasing calorie intake by another 300 calories per day. On the other hand, if you are gaining more than 2 pounds per month, consider removing 10% (300 calories) from your daily intake.

HOW MUCH WEIGHT SHOULD YOU BE GAINING EACH WEEK?

Here's an example of how much weight you should gain after training for a year and more. This is from the Lean Muscle Mass Gain Model developed by Lyle McDonald.

Years Training:

1 year	20-25 lbs (2 lbs per month)
2 years	10-12 lbs (1 lbs per month)
3 years	5-6 lbs (0.5 lbs per month)
4 years	2-3 lbs (not worth calculating)

According to this diagram, your weight gain should decrease yearly. Within 4 years of consistent training, you would be able to develop enough muscle that all you need to do then is to maintain your calorie intake and exercise routine.

Lean muscle building macros: How to split calories between protein, carbs and fats:

Protein

As a healthy adult with consistent weight training, you are recommended to follow this daily protein intake:

0.8 to 1.5 grams for every pound of your body weight.

A study recently published in the Journal of Applied Physiology revealed that subjects who ate at least 20 grams of protein spread out over six meals and snacks, lost more body fat, and increased lean mass, more than the average male. And this is without any training at all, accomplished only via diet!

The study showed that protein synthesis was about 25% higher for those subjects who at least 30 grams of protein in each of their three meals, as opposed to those who had most of their protein during dinner.

I recommend that you eat protein six times a day spreading your intake over the day. Six full meals may sound excessive but you need to do this especially in the beginning stages of your program.

(1 gram of protein = 4 calories)

Fat

The recommended fat intake for average adults is about 25% of the total calorie intake.

(1 gram of fat= 9 calories)

So let's say your calorie maintenance level is 2,000 calories per day and 25% of that is 500. That means you should divide 500 by 9 to get the amount of fat that you need per day. According to this example, you will need to consume about 55 grams of fat each day. You can find 'healthy fat' contents in fish, nuts, and seeds.

Carbohydrates

Your ideal carb intake must come from healthy foods like fruits and vegetables, brown or white rice, sweet potatoes, and different types of beans. Unless you have a problem with digesting grains, you may also find the carbs you need in whole grain products.
After you have worked out how many calories you need from your protein and fats, the calories left should come from carbohydrates.

(1g of carbohydrates = 4 calories)

Here, I'm going to show you every step clearly. Let's say I weigh 175 lbs and my calorie maintenance level per day is 2,250 calories. Here's how I would create my diet plan with this number.

1.   Since I want to build muscle, that means I need to add 10% more calories to my CML. My calorie maintenance level is 2,250 calories so I would need to consume 2,500 calories each day.
2.   Since I weigh 175 lbs, that means I need to consume 175 grams of protein per day. Now, a gram of protein contains 4 calories. So if I multiply 175 by 4, that

means I will already consume 700 calories with 175 grams of protein.

3.   Then, I need to take about 25% of my calorie intake from fat. Since my maintenance calorie level is 2,500 per day, 25% of that is 625. Since I can consume 9 calories in 1 gram of fat, then I would need to consume about 69 grams of fat each day.

4.   By this time, I already have 700 calories from protein and 625 calories from fat, which gives me a total of 1325 calories already. Since I need to take 2,500 calories per day, I still need to consume additional 1117 calories.

5.   Now, my remaining calorie need should come from carbs. Since I can consume 4 calories in 1 gram of carbs, I would need to consume about 294 grams of carbs each day.

So that's it. You have learned the most important parts of the sample diet plan. According to the given example, here's how my diet plan should appear:

1.   2500 calories
2.   175 grams protein
3.   69 grams fats
4.   294 grams carbs

Remember that this diet plan is only an example. You need to compute your own calorie maintenance level in order to know the appropriate measurement of protein, fat, carb, and calorie that you need to consume each day.

4
EATING TO BURN FAT AND GET SHREDDED

In the previous chapter, I detailed how you should be able to gain muscle. In this chapter, I will explain how to lose weight which is helpful if you need to lose fat before you start bodybuilding, or if you are looking to get shredded.

WHY PEOPLE CAN'T LOSE WEIGHT

1.   You will not lose weight if you consume excess calories. In order to lose weight, you have to burn more calories and eat less.
2.   A hormonal imbalance could be the culprit. Medical professionals discovered that an under-active thyroid can cause weight gain.
3.   Some medications may cause you to gain weight. If you are taking antihistamines or antidepressants, it can be difficult for you to lose weight. If you are currently on medication and you think it might be the reason why you can't lose weight, speak to your doctor about alternatives.
4.   You can't lose weight if you're relying solely on exercise.
5.   A slow metabolism can make it hard for you to lose weight.

HOW TO CALCULATE CALORIE INTAKE TO BURN FAT

If you want to lose weight, you should have a calorie deficit. This could be done by reducing consumption of food or by engaging in more physical activities. If your goal is to get shredded, you'll need an effective exercise routine.
This weight loss should be healthy; you should not starve yourself or speed up weight loss. You will still need to consume from the entire food groups so you will maintain proper body function and stay healthy.

If you want to lose fat, you will need to eat 20% below your CML.

You should aim to lose between ½ pound to 2 pounds per week and no more. The losses should be closer to 2 pounds if you are starting off at a high BMI, or you have a lot of weight to lose. If you are losing less than ½ pound, or are not losing any weight at all, you need to reduce your intake of calories by another 10%.

Note that someone who is obese, should eat less carbohydrates and fat in proportion to their total calories. Carbohydrates tend to play a big role in weight gain, so those who are looking to lose weight should go for higher portions of protein over carbs and fat.

Important points to remember when shredding:

1.   First, don't forget to maintain your protein intake. If your protein intake is low, chances are you'll also lose your muscle mass along the way.
2.   Try alternating between low carb and medium carb days.
3.   Lastly, drink about a gallon of water each day. Water can keep you healthy and hydrated.

Tracking Your Progress:

As previously stated, choose a common time every week to weigh yourself and keep a record of these weights so you can see how much your gaining/losing. This way you can adjust your diet accordingly. The most beneficial way of tracking progress is by looking in the mirror though! The scales and tape measures can only tell you so much.

SAMPLE MEAL PLAN

Nutrition Facts:
Protein – 40%
Fat – 30%
Carbohydrate – 30%
Calorie – 2,200

Breakfast (420 Calories)
0.5 large banana
250 ml skimmed milk
48 g peanut butter

Morning Snack (350 Calories)
1 apple
40 g almonds

Lunch (350 calories)
200 grams broccoli
200 grams carrots
10 grams almond
1 piece of chicken fillet

Pre-Workout Snack (330 Calories)
25 grams whey protein
1 apple
375 ml skimmed milk

Post-Workout Snack (350 Calories)
250 ml skimmed milk
2 50 grams whey protein
0.5 large banana

Dinner (380 calories)
200 grams green beans
1.5 salmon fillet
1 tablespoon olive oil

5
PRE & POST WORKOUT NUTRITION

Your body needs fuel in order to move. This is why pre-workout meals or drinks are very important.

• You need nutrients to boost your energy, depending on your workout activity.
• Eating the proper nutrients after your training will help your body improve in performance and recover quickly.

Protein synthesis is a crucial process in lean muscle building, and in fact, post workout meals focus primarily on making sure that it occurs. To those who have been lifting for a long time, protein synthesis peaks way earlier. Long-time body-builders and weight lifters experience it 4 hours after working out. If you are a complete beginner to muscle building, it might take around 6 hours, or even longer. According to a study conducted in 2013, the results of which were published in the Journal of the International Society of Sports Nutrition, muscles of the average person are most receptive to protein 4-6 hours after working out.

This is why protein intake before and after a rigorous workout is crucial. This means that you should have a protein-rich meal 2-3 hours before working out, and then another one 1-2 hours after training. You need protein to repair your tissues, and to get muscle growth going. Your body automatically reverts to 'repair mode' if these nutrients are readily available.

Protein synthesis slows down during sleep, so you should eat something as soon as you wake up if you're planning to train.

Sample Post Workout Meal

1.   Protein Pancake
Ingredients:
1/8 teaspoon baking powder
½ cup cottage cheese
½ teaspoon vanilla extract
½ cup oats
4 egg whites

How to make:

Mix all ingredients and cook as you would any pancakes. Once cooked, top the pancakes with berries or fresh banana slices.

2.   Crackers With Tuna
Ingredients:
½ cup of crushed crackers, whole grain
1 can of tuna, yellow fin

How to make:
Mix all ingredients and add pepper, pickles and mustard to taste.

3.   Oats
Ingredients:
½ cup almonds, dried or frozen
½ cup rolled oats
1 scoop whey protein

How to make:
Mix all ingredients and refrigerate overnight. Add cinnamon for added taste.

So, let's get started!

Now you know how many calories your should be eating, the recommended percentages of proteins, fats and carbs and have stocked up your kitchen - you're ready to go!

The rest of this book is dedicated to providing you with 150 recipes that you can use whether you're looking to build muscle or get shredded. They are easy to cook, taste delicious and won't get boring.

So get out of the rut of boiled chicken and raw eggs and try your hand at these delicious meals.

If your looking to shred, simply keep track of the calories you're consuming. All the meals have been created to be lean and fresh and so are suitable for bulking and shredding.

Apps like myfitnesspal can help you keep track of your calories and even show you the ratio of fats, carbs and proteins you have consumed. But I've included a breakdown of all the nutritional information for each dish to help you total it up and make your life easy.

If you need to adjust anything, simply adjust! Add extra proteins to recipes for higher protein count and reduce the carbohydrates you pair with the meals to lower carb content.

I wish you all the best on your bodybuilding journey - it always starts with the first step!

BREAKFAST

MIGHTY QUINOA BREAKFAST CEREAL

SERVES 2 / PREP TIME: 2 MINUTES / COOK TIME: 20 MINUTES

Start your protein kick early in the morning without having to down the raw eggs!

---

1 1/2 CUP QUINOA

1 CUP BLACKBERRIES

3 CUP WATER

1/4 TSP GROUND NUTMEG

1/2 TSP VANILLA EXTRACT

---

1. Get a pan and combine all of the ingredients, cooking over medium to high heat until boiling.
2. Once boiling, cover and simmer for 15 minutes or until the quinoa is soft and the liquid has been absorbed.
3. Pour into serving bowls and enjoy.

Per Serving: 527 Calories , 22G Protein, 96G Carbohydrates, 9G Fat

BOUNTY OATS

SERVES 2 / PREP TIME: 2 MINUTES / COOK TIME: 10 MINUTES

Start your day right with coconut and chocolatey oats.

2 CUPS WHOLEMEAL OATS	1 SCOOP CHOCOLATE PROTEIN POWDER
1 TBSP MILLED CHIA SEEDS	1 TBSP COCONUT SHAVINGS
3 CUPS COCONUT MILK	6 STRAWBERRIES (OR ANY FRUIT OF YOUR CHOICE)

1. In a pan mix the oats, and coconut milk.
2. Heat on a medium heat and then simmer until the oats are fully cooked through (5-10 minutes).
3. Pour into your favorite breakfast bowl and stir in the protein powder, strawberries and milled chia seeds on top.
4. If you've got a sweet tooth or fancy an extra treat, try adding cacao or a drizzle of honey to serve.

Per Serving: 550 Calories, 22G Protein, 64G Carbohydrates, 24G Fat

BRAWNY BUCKWHEAT BREAKFAST GRANOLA

SERVES 4 / PREP TIME: 10 MINUTES / COOK TIME: 45 MINUTES

Homemade power cereal!

---

1 CUP WHOLEMEAL OR STEEL CUT OATS

1/3 CUP BUCKWHEAT

2 CUPS WATER

1/3 CUP SUNFLOWER SEEDS

1/3 CUP PUMPKIN SEEDS

1/2 CUP ALMONDS

1/3 CUP BLUEBERRIES

1/2 CUP OF PEELED AND FINELY CHOPPED APPLES

1 TBSP COCONUT OIL

1 TSP GINGER (FRESH AND GRATED)

---

1. Preheat the oven to 350°f/180°c/Gas Mark 4.
2. Meanwhile mix the oats, buckwheat, nuts and seeds into a bowl.
3. Put the berries, apples, coconut oil and water to cover in a pan; cover and simmer for 10-15 minutes on a medium-high heat until the fruits are soft to touch. Then stir in the ginger.
4. Add the fruit mixture to a blender until smooth.
5. Mix the fruits with the buckwheat.
6. Grease a baking tray with coconut oil and then spread the granola mixture on top using a knife or spatula to create a thin layer. Bake for 45 minutes.
7. Stir the mixture every 15 minutes so it doesn't burn. When crispy all over, remove the tray and allow to cool.
8. Serve as a crispy breakfast treat alongside low fat yogurt and fresh fruit if desired.

Per Serving: 665 Calories, 22G Protein, 77G Carbohydrates, 36G Fat

SIZZLING SAUSAGE PATTIES

SERVES 4 / PREP TIME: 8 MINUTES / COOK TIME: 15 - 20 MINUTES

These patties are made with lean ground pork and no added preservatives! Enjoy.

18OZ OF LEAN GROUND PORK	1/4 TSP CHOPPED OREGANO
2 TSP FRESH CHOPPED SAGE LEAVES	1 TBSP EXTRA VIRGIN OLIVE OIL
1 TSP CHOPPED THYME	4 EGGS
1 TSP GROUND BLACK PEPPER	
1/4 TSP GROUND NUTMEG	
1/4 TSP CAYENNE PEPPER	

1. Get a mixing bowl and add all of the ingredients.
2. Mix with a spoon or blender until blended and form 8 patties using the palms of your hands to shape.
3. Heat the oil in a skillet, over a medium heat and cook the patties for 9 minutes one side and 9 on the other side until they're browned and cooked through.

Per Serving: 440 Calories, 17G Protein, 31G Carbohydrates, 29G Fat

GET-FIT FRITTATA

SERVES 2 / PREP TIME: 10 MINUTES / COOK TIME: 30 MINUTES

Great for a quick breakfast at home or in a Tupperware for after training!

---

1 TBSP COCONUT OR EXTRA VIRGIN OLIVE OIL

4 EGGS

1 SWEET POTATO, PEELED AND SLICED USING POTATO SLICER OR SHARP KNIFE.

1 PEELED AND SLICED RED BELL PEPPER

2 TSP OREGANO

1/2 PEELED AND SLICED ZUCCHINI

1 TSP CRACKED BLACK PEPPER

1 CUP SPINACH LEAVES/ARUGULA

---

1. Preheat broiler on a medium heat.
2. Heat the oil in a skillet under the broiler until hot.
3. Spread the potato slices across the skillet and cooking for 8-10 minutes or until soft.
4. Add the zucchini and red bell pepper to the skillet and cook for a further 5 minutes.
5. Meanwhile, whisk the eggs and oregano in a separate bowl, and season to taste before pouring mixture over the veggies in the skillet.
6. Cook for 10 minutes on a low heat until golden.
7. Remove and turn over onto a plate or serving board.
8. Serve with a side of spinach leaves or arugula.
9. Cut the frittata into slices to serve.

Per Serving: 337 Calories, 17G Protein, 33G Carbohydrates, 15G Fat

EGGS IN AVOCADOS!

SERVES 2 / PREP TIME: 2 MINUTES / COOK TIME: 4 MINUTES

Poach the egg and float it in its own avocado boat; full of healthy fats and protein to start your day.

---

2 RIPE AVOCADO

4 EGGS

1 TBSP WHITE WINE VINEGAR

---

1. Place a large pan of water on a high heat and boil.
2. Once boiling add white wine vinegar (don't worry if you don't have it, it just helps with the poaching).
3. Lower the heat to a simmer and crack the eggs in. Top tip: do it quickly and from a height to get a nice round shape.
4. Stir the water ever now and then around the eggs to keep them moving and cook for 2 minutes for a very runny yolk; 2-4 minutes for a soft to firm yolk and 5 for a hard yolk.
5. Whilst cooking, prepare your avocado by cutting through to the stone lengthways around the whole of the fruit.
6. Use your palms on each side to twist the avocado and it should come away into 2 halves. Using your knife, carefully wedge it into the stone and pull to remove the stone. Alternatively, cut around the stone with the knife and use the sharp end to coax it out.
7. Use your avocado halves as a dish for the eggs and serve.
8. Season to taste! Yum.

Per Serving: 334 Calories, 14G Protein, 18G Carbohydrates, 37G Fat

BRILLIANT BREAKFAST BIRCHER

SERVES 2 / PREP TIME: 2 MINUTES (REST OVERNIGHT IF POSSIBLE) / COOK TIME: NA

Greek yogurt is high in protein and a staple bodybuilding ingredient! Tastes great for breakfast or as a snack.

1 CUP OF WHOLEGRAIN OATS

2 TANGERINES, PEELED AND SLICED

1/2 CUP PINEAPPLE, CHOPPED

16 OZ. LOW FAT GREEK YOGURT

1 TBSP COCONUT SHAVINGS

1. Mix the oats and fruit with the yogurt and allow to soak for as long as possible (overnight is best).
2. Serve and top with coconut shavings – the oats should be nice and mushy and will have soaked up the flavors of the fruit.

Per Serving: 395 Calories, 28G Protein, 52G Carbohydrates, 10G Fat

MIGHTY MINI MEATLOAVES

SERVES 2 / PREP TIME: 10 MINUTES / COOK TIME: 30 MINUTES

Scrumptious, meaty treats.

---

1 CUP LEAN GROUND TURKEY

1 CUP SKINLESS GROUND CHICKEN

1/2 CUP COCONUT MILK

1 MINCED GARLIC CLOVE

1/4 CUP PARSLEY

1 TBSP PAPRIKA

SPRINKLE OF BLACK PEPPER

1 TSP COCONUT OIL

---

1. Preheat the oven to 400°f/200°c/Gas Mark 6.
2. Mix turkey, chicken, garlic, parsley, paprika, and coconut milk together, mixing until the ingredients hold.
3. Season with black pepper to taste.
4. Line a muffin tin with coconut oil and divide the mixture into each hole.
5. Bake in the oven for 30 minutes or until the meat is cooked through.
6. Serve hot!

Per Serving: 495 Calories, 53G Protein, 2G Carbohydrates, 29G Fat

SCORE-BOARD SCOTCH EGGS

SERVES 2 /   PREP TIME: 10 MINUTES   / COOK TIME: 25 MINUTES

A great addition to meal prep day - just pop in your containers for a breakfast treat or post-workout fuel!

---

16 OZ LEAN GROUND CHICKEN

1/2 TSP BLACK PEPPER

1/2 TSP CAYENNE PEPPER

1/2 TSP PAPRIKA

1/2 TSP CLOVES

1/2 CUP FRESH PARSLEY, FINELY CHOPPED

1/2 TBSP DRIED CHIVES

1 CLOVE GARLIC, FINELY CHOPPED

4 FREE RANGE EGGS, BOILED AND PEELED

---

1. Preheat the oven to 375°F/190°C/Gas Mark 5.
2. Cover a baking sheet with parchment paper.
3. Combine the chicken with the paprika, cayenne pepper, pepper, cloves, chives, parsley and garlic in a mixing bowl and mix with your hands until thoroughly mixed.
4. Divide the mixture into 4 circular shapes with the palms of your hands.
5. Flatten each one into a pancake shape using the backs of your hands or a rolling pin.
6. Wrap the meat pancake around 1 egg, until it's covered. (You can moisten the meat with water first to help prevent it from sticking to your hands).
7. Bake in the oven for 25 minutes or until brown and crisp – check the meat is cooked through with a knife before serving.

Per Serving: 424 Calories, 47G Protein, 4G Carbohydrates, 22G Fat

EPIC EGG MUFFINS

SERVES 3 / PREP TIME: 15 MINUTES / COOK TIME: 25 MINUTES

Energizing and delicious!

8OZ COOKED SKINLESS CHICKEN	1/3 CUP BELL PEPPER, DICED
1/3 CUP RED ONION, DICED	1 TSP DRIED TARRAGON
1/3 CUP GREEN BELL PEPPER, DICED	6 LARGE EGGS

---

1. Line a muffin pan with 6 wrappers.
2. Mix vegetables together in a separate bowl.
3. Next, spoon the vegetable mixture and chicken pieces into the muffin trays up to about 2/3 full, allowing room for the eggs.
4. Beat the eggs with the thyme in a separate bowl or jug.
5. Pour beaten eggs into each muffin tray - leave 1cm gap at the top.
6. Place the muffin tray in the oven and bake for approximately 25 minutes or until eggs are cooked through.
7. Remove egg muffins and serve.

Per Serving: 232 Calories, 31G Protein, 6G Carbohydrates, 10G Fat

TURKEY BACON OMELETTE

SERVES 2 / PREP TIME: 5 MINUTES / COOK TIME: 15 MINUTES

Protein rich and easy to prepare.

---

1 TBSP EXTRA VIRGIN OLIVE OIL	2 TBSP WATER
1/2 LEEK, DICED	PINCH OF BLACK PEPPER
8 OZ TURKEY BACON	2 LARGE EGG WHITES
1 GREEN ONION, DICED	2 LARGE EGGS

---

1. Heat olive oil in a skillet over a medium to high heat.
2. Sauté the vegetables and turkey bacon for 4-5 minutes.
3. Using a whisk, mix together the egg, egg whites, pepper and water together in a separate bowl.
4. Pour the eggs into the skillet over the vegetables and cook for 5-6 minutes until the edges begin to set.
5. Use a spatula to gently lift the edges of the omelette and turn over in the pan.
6. Fold the omelette in half and continue cooking for 3-4 minutes.
7. Remove omelette from the pan and cut in half to serve.

Per Serving: 236 Calories, 15G Protein, 6G Carbohydrates, 15G Fat

BANANA & HAZELNUT OATMEAL

SERVES 2 / PREP TIME: 5 MINUTES / COOK TIME: 5 MINUTES

Wholesome and tasty!

---

1 CUP WHOLEGRAIN OATS

2 CUPS ALMOND MILK

2 SCOOP VANILLA PROTEIN POWDER

2 BANANAS, CHOPPED

1/4 CUP CHOPPED HAZELNUTS

---

1. Add the oats and milk into a large bowl, stir and place in the microwave for two minutes.
2. Add the banana, whey protein and chopped hazelnuts to the oats and stir well.
3. Serve warm.

Per Serving: 533 Calories, 27G Protein, 63G Carbohydrates, 17G Fat

PERFECT PANCAKES

SERVES 2 / PREP TIME: 10 MINUTES / COOK TIME: 25 MINUTES

A great addition to meal prep day - just pop in your containers for a breakfast treat or post-workout fuel!

---

6 EGG WHITES

1/2 CUP OF ROLLED OATS

1 TSP FLAXSEED OIL

1 TSP OF CINNAMON

1 TSP OF STEVIA

1/2 CUP MIXED BERRIES

1/2 CUP GREEK YOGURT

---

1. Blend all ingredients in a food processor until smooth.
2. Spray a pan or skillet with cooking spray and heat over a medium heat.
3. Pour roughly 1/2 of the pancake batter into the pan and cook for 1-2 minutes. Flip the pancake and cook for another 30 seconds.
4. Once done, remove your tasty pancake.
5. Use the same method for the rest of your batter.
6. Serve with extra fruit of your choice.

Per Serving: 262 Calories, 19G Protein, 27G Carbohydrates, 9G Fat

WORKOUT WAFFLES

SERVES 2 / PREP TIME: 10 MINUTES / COOK TIME: 25 MINUTES

You can still enjoy waffles whilst training with this recipe.

---

4 EGG WHITES

1 SCOOP OF CHOCOLATE PROTEIN POWDER

1/2 CUP OF ROLLED OATS

1 TSP OF BAKING POWDER

½ TSP OF STEVIA

1/2 CUP STRAWBERRIES TO SERVE

---

1. Add all the ingredients into a blender and blend.
2. Add the mixture to a waffle iron and bake.
3. Serve with fresh strawberries and enjoy!

Per Serving: 270 Calories, 35G Protein, 23G Carbohydrates, 4G Fat

STRENGTHENING SPINACH SCRAMBLE

SERVES 2 / PREP TIME: 10 MINUTES / COOK TIME: 25 MINUTES

Healthy fats and protein combine in this tasty and fast breakfast.

2 EGGS	1 CUP OF BABY SPINACH
2 EGG WHITES	4OZ TURKEY PIECES, COOKED
1 TSP OREGANO	1/2 CHOPPED ONION
1 TSP PARSLEY	1 GARLIC CLOVE, DICED
1 TSP SESAME SEEDS	1 TSP OF OLIVE OIL
	1 AVOCADO

1. Add oil to a skillet and place over a medium to high heat.
2. Add the chopped onion and garlic and cook for 5 minutes or until soft.
3. Add the turkey pieces and continue to cook for 3-4 minutes.
4. Whisk the eggs and egg whites in a separate bowl and add oregano and parsley.
5. Add the eggs to the pan and stir through.
6. Continue to stir for 5-6 minutes or until eggs are cooked through.
7. Add the spinach to the pan and stir through for 2-3 minutes or until wilted.
8. Peel and slice the avocado and serve on the side of the scrambled eggs.
9. Sprinkle with the sesame seeds and a little black pepper.
10. Enjoy!

Per Serving: 411 Calories, 30G Protein, 13G Carbohydrates, 35G Fat

SWEET POTATO PANCAKES

SERVES 2 / PREP TIME: 10 MINUTES / COOK TIME: 25 MINUTES

Sweet and savoury pancakes - the sweet potatoes will keep you going for longer.

---

1 SWEET POTATO

1 TSP OLIVE OIL

1 EGG

4 EGG WHITES

1 CUP FAT-FREE GREEK YOGURT

1/2 CUP OATS

1 TSP MAPLE SYRUP

1 BANANA, SLICED

---

1. Rinse sweet potato and add to a microwaveable sandwich bag with olive oil.
2. Microwave for 12 minutes.
3. Remove and allow to cool before removing the skin from the sweet potato with a sharp knife.
4. If you don't have a microwave, simply pierce sweet potato with a fork and add to a hot oven for 20-30 minutes or until soft.
5. Put the oats into a blender and blend to a fine powder, then place into a bowl.
6. Place the sweet potato in the blender and blend until smooth, and then mix with the powdered oats.
7. Add the egg, egg whites, maple syrup and yogurt and stir well.
8. Spray a pan with cooking spray and place over a medium heat.
9. Pour roughly a quarter of the batter into the pan and cook for 1-2 minutes.
10. Flip the pancake and cook for another 30 seconds.
11. Enjoy hot with sliced banana to serve (optional).
12. Use the same method for the rest of your batter.

Per Serving: 376 Calories, 16G Protein, 45G Carbohydrates, 15G Fat

CLASSIC STEAK, MUSHROOM & EGGS

SERVES 2 / PREP TIME: 10 MINUTES / COOK TIME: 25 MINUTES

It's a cliché for a reason!

2X 6OZ OF RUMP BEEF STEAKS

1 TSP PAPRIKA

1 TSP MIXED DRIED HERBS

2 EGGS

1 LARGE BEEF TOMATO, SLICED IN HALF

I LARGE FIELD MUSHROOM, SLICED IN HALF

---

1. Heat the broiler on high.
2. Sprinkle paprika and herbs over each side of the steaks.
3. Add the steaks to a baking tray/griddle pan and place under the broiler.
4. Cook using the following approximate timings for each side:
5. 2 minutes = rare
6. 3-4 minutes = medium
7. 5-6 minutes = well done
8. Whilst the steak is cooking, add the tomato and mushroom to the pan, turning once through cooking.
9. Remove the steak and vegetables from the pan once done and allow to rest.
10. Crack the eggs onto the pan/tray and allow to cook for 4-5 minutes or until cooked through (3-4 minutes for a runny yolk and add a couple of minutes for a hard yolk).
11. Plate up and serve!

Per Serving: 470 Calories, 60G Protein, 6G Carbohydrates, 23G Fat

PUMPIN' PUMPKIN PANCAKES

SERVES 2 / PREP TIME: 10 MINUTES / COOK TIME: 25 MINUTES

Savoury , tasty and healthy pancakes.

FLESH FROM 1/4 DESEEDED PUMPKIN

2 TBSP WATER

4 EGGS

3 EGG WHITES

1 TSP OF BLACK PEPPER

1 TSP GLUTEN-FREE BAKING SODA

2 TBSP COCONUT OIL

1 TBSP RAW HONEY

1 HANDFUL WALNUTS

---

1. In a blender or food processor, blend the pumpkin flesh together with water to form a smooth pulp.
2. Now add the eggs, freshly ground pepper, 1 tbsp of coconut oil, and baking soda to the pumpkin mix and blend until smooth.
3. Heat a large pan on a medium heat with the 1 tbsp of coconut oil.
4. Pour into the pan into individual rounded pancakes.
5. Lift the mixture with a spatula and then flip.
6. Cook for 3 minutes on either side.
7. Plate and serve with walnuts and honey.

Per Serving: 435 Calories, 21G Protein, 14G Carbohydrates, 33G Fat

BODYBUILDER'S BANANA PANCAKES

SERVES 2 / PREP TIME: 10 MINUTES / COOK TIME: 25 MINUTES

Get 1 of your 5 a day with these tasty pancakes.

---

2 SCOOPS UNFLAVORED PROTEIN POWDER

1/2 CUP WHOLE GRAIN FLOUR

1/4 CUP ROLLED OATS

1 BANANA, MASHED

1 LARGE EGG

1 TBSP ALMOND MILK

1 TSP RAW HONEY

1 CUP STRAWBERRIES

---

1. Thoroughly mix the protein powder, flour and oats in a large bowl.
2. Add the banana, egg and almond milk and mix in well.
3. Add frying spray to a non-stick skillet and heat over a medium heat.
4. Pour 1/4 batter into the pan and allow to sit for 2-3 minutes before flipping.
5. Repeat for the rest of the batter and serve 2 pancakes each with honey and strawberries on top.

Per Serving: 400 Calories, 28G Protein, 55G Carbohydrates, 7G Fat

CHERRY PROTEIN PORRIDGE

SERVES 2 / PREP TIME: 10 MINUTES / COOK TIME: 25 MINUTES

Warm & sweet!

---

2 CUPS ROLLED OATS

1/2 CUP CHERRIES

2 SCOOPS VANILLA PROTEIN POWDER

4 CUPS ALMOND MILK

---

1. Mix the oats with the almond milk in a large bowl.
2. Add to a pan on the stove over a medium heat until it starts to bubble slightly but not boil.
3. Alternatively place in the microwave for 1.5 minutes.
4. Remove from the pan and return to the large bowl.
5. Stir in the protein powder until there are no lumps left.
6. Top with cherries and serve.

Per Serving: 370 Calories, 27G Protein, 41G Carbohydrates, 11G Fat

POULTRY

ARTICHOKE & TOMATO CHICKEN BAKE

SERVES 2 / PREP TIME: 5 MINUTES / COOK TIME: 40 MINUTES

A taste of the Mediterranean!

4X SKINLESS CHICKEN THIGHS	1 CUP HOMEMADE CHICKEN STOCK
1 ONION, ROUGHLY CHOPPED	1 BAY LEAF
2 GARLIC CLOVES, CHOPPED	A PINCH OF BLACK PEPPER
2 CANS CHOPPED TOMATOES	1 CUP BROWN RICE
1 TBSP BALSAMIC VINEGAR	
1/2 CUP JARRED ARTICHOKES	

1. Preheat oven to 375°F/190 °C/Gas Mark 5.
2. Add the onion, garlic, chopped tomatoes, artichoke, chicken stock, balsamic vinegar and the bay leaf to a baking dish and cover.
3. Place in the oven for 35-40 minutes or until chicken is thoroughly cooked.
4. Meanwhile add the rice to a pan of water and bring to the boil.
5. Lower the heat and simmer for 20 minutes or until most of the water is absorbed.
6. Drain, return the lid and steam for 5 minutes.
7. Plate up and serve with a pinch of black pepper and brown rice.

Per Serving: 695 Calories, 49G Protein, 55G Carbohydrates, 33G Fat

CAJUN CHICKEN

SERVES 2 / PREP TIME: 5 MINUTES / COOK TIME: 35 MINUTES

Scrumptious!

2X SKINLESS CHICKEN BREASTS, SLICED

1 RED ONION, CHOPPED

1 GREEN PEPPER, CHOPPED

2 GARLIC CLOVES, CRUSHED

1 TSP CAYENNE PEPPER

1 TSP CHILI POWDER

1/4 TSP CHILI POWDER

1 TSP DRIED OREGANO

1 TSP DRIED THYME

1 CUP BROWN RICE

1 TBSP EXTRA VIRGIN OLIVE OIL

1/2 CAN CHOPPED TOMATOES

1 CUP HOMEMADE CHICKEN STOCK

---

1. Mix the spices and herbs in a separate bowl to form your Cajun spice mix.
2. Grab a large pan and add the olive oil, heating on a medium heat.
3. Coat the chicken strips in the cajun spices.
4. Add the chicken and brown each side for around 4-5 minutes. Place to one side.
5. Add the onion to the pan and fry until soft.
6. Add the garlic and green pepper to the pan and cook for around 5 minutes.
7. Add the brown rice along with the chopped tomatoes, chicken and chicken stock to the pan.
8. Cover the pan and allow to simmer for around 25 minutes or until the rice is soft.
9. Serve hot.

Per Serving: 560 Calories, 65G Protein, 40G Carbohydrates, 15G Fat

CHICKEN BURGERS & GUACAMOLE

SERVES 2 / PREP TIME: 5 MINUTES / COOK TIME: 35 MINUTES

Healthy chicken burgers with wholemeal pittas.

2X SKINLESS CHICKEN BREASTS

1 TSP OREGANO

1 TSP PAPRIKA

1 TSP GARLIC SALT

2 X WHOLEMEAL PITTA BREADS

1 AVOCADO

1/4 CUP GREEK YOGURT

1/2 LIME, JUICED

1/4 CUP SPINACH LEAVES, WASHED

1 TOMATO, SLICED

---

1. Preheat the broiler to a medium high heat.
2. Slice the chicken breasts in half lengthways.
3. Mix the herbs and spices together and sprinkle over the chicken breasts.
4. Add the chicken to a baking tray and broil for 20-25 minutes or until thoroughly cooked through.
5. Meanwhile, peel and slice the avocado and add to the natural yogurt with the lime juice. Use your fork to mush these together to form the guacamole. Season with a little black pepper.
6. Lightly toast the pitta breads and then stuff each with a chicken breast, spinach leaves, tomato and a dollop of guacamole.
7. Enjoy!

Per Serving: 410 Calories, 35G Protein, 55G Carbohydrates, 17G Fat

DIVINE DUCK BREASTS

SERVES 2 / PREP TIME: 4 MINUTES / COOK TIME: 20 MINUTES

Chinese spiced duck breasts.

---

1 TSP COCONUT OIL

2 DUCK BREASTS, SKIN REMOVED

2 GREEN ONIONS, SLICED

3 GARLIC CLOVES, MINCED

2 TSP GINGER, GRATED

1 TSP NUTMEG

1 TSP CLOVES

1 ORANGE – ZEST AND JUICE (RESERVE THE WEDGES)

2 BOK OR PAK CHOI PLANTS, LEAVES SEPARATED

---

1. Slice the duck breasts into strips and add to a dry hot pan, cooking for 5-7 minutes on each side or until cooked through to your liking.
2. Remove to one side.
3. Add oil to a clean pan and sauté the onions with the ginger, garlic and the rest of the spices for 1 minute.
4. Add the juice and zest of the orange and continue to sauté for 3-5 minutes.
5. Add the duck and bok choi and heat through until wilted and duck is piping hot.
6. Serve and garnish with the orange segments.

Per Serving: 230 Calories, 28G Protein, 15G Carbohydrates, 17G Fat

TASTY TURKEY BURGERS

SERVES 2 / PREP TIME: 5 MINUTES / COOK TIME: 35 MINUTES

Lean and mouthwatering!

---

10 OZ LEAN GROUND TURKEY MEAT	1 TSP DRY MUSTARD
1 WHITE ONION, MINCED	2 TBSP OLIVE OIL
1 CARROT, SHREDDED	PINCH OF BLACK PEPPER TO TASTE
2 CELERY STALKS, FINELY CHOPPED	2 WHOLEGRAIN BUNS
1 TBSP PARSLEY	1/2 CUP ARUGULA
1 TSP CILANTRO	

---

1. Pre-heat oven to 390°F/200 °C/Gas Mark 6.
2. Add the vegetables in a bowl with the olive oil, pepper and herbs and then mix well.
3. Add in the meat and mix with wet hands to create two burgers.
4. Place the burgers on a lightly oiled baking tray and bake in the oven for 25-30 minutes or until meat is cooked through (flip half way).
5. Turn up the broiler and broil for the last 5 minutes for a golden and crispy edge.
6. Serve in the buns with arugula.

Per Serving: 230 Calories, 28G Protein, 15G Carbohydrates, 17G Fat

OVEN-BAKED CHICKEN THIGHS

SERVES 4 / PREP TIME: 10 MINUTES / COOK TIME: 35 MINUTES

An exciting take on your usual bland chicken meals.

---

4 CHICKEN THIGHS

2 SWEET POTATOES, PEELED AND CHOPPED

2 RED ONIONS, CHOPPED

1/2 CUP GREEK YOGURT

1 TSP PAPRIKA

FOR THE MARINADE:

1 RED PEPPER, DICED

1 TSP DRIED RED CHILLI,

1 GARLIC CLOVE, MINCED

1 TSP BASIL, CHOPPED

1 TBSP TOMATO PURÉE (NO ADDED SALT OR SUGAR)

1 TBSP EXTRA VIRGIN OLIVE OIL

---

1. Pre-heat oven to 375°F/190 °C/Gas Mark 5.
2. In a bowl, combine the ingredients for the marinade.
3. Coat the chicken with the mixture, cover and leave to one side.
4. Pour the chicken pieces, onions and sweet potato, with the leftover marinade juices over a baking tray and place in the oven for 35 minutes or until the chicken is thoroughly cooked through.
5. Add the yogurt to a serving bowl and sprinkle paprika over the top.
6. Plate up the chicken and vegetables with the yogurt dressing.

Top tip: double up the ingredients for the marinade and use later for meat, fish or even vegetables.

Per Serving: 230 Calories, 28G Protein, 15G Carbohydrates, 17G Fat

NOURISHING NUTTY NOODLES

SERVES 2 / PREP TIME: 10 MINUTES / COOK TIME: 20 MINUTES

These are great for lunch or dinner and taste like a cheat meal!

---

2 SKINLESS CHICKEN BREASTS, SLICED

1 CUP NOODLES

1 CARROT, CHOPPED

1 LIME, JUICED

1 TBSP CASHEW NUTS, CRUSHED

2 TSP COCONUT OIL

1/2 CUP BROCCOLI FLORETS

1/2 CUP MUSHROOMS

---

1. Heat 1 tsp oil on a medium heat in a skillet.
2. Sauté the chicken breasts for about 10-15 minutes or until cooked through.
3. While cooking the chicken, place the noodles, carrots and broccoli in a pot of boiling water for 5 minutes. Drain.
4. In a bowl, mix together 1 tsp oil, lime juice and crushed cashew nuts to make your dressing.
5. Add all of the ingredients to the dressing and toss through.
6. Serve warm straight away or chill in airtight container for a go-to lunch.

Per Serving: 403 Calories, 31G Protein, 27G Carbohydrates, 18G Fat

TRAINING TURKEY KEBABS

**SERVES 4 / PREP TIME: 10 MINUTES (MARINATE AS LONG AS POSSIBLE) /
COOK TIME: 25 MINUTES**

Turkey is lean and full of protein and tastes delicious in this kebab recipe with salsa.

FOR THE CHICKEN:	FOR THE SALSA:
1 LEMON, JUICED	1 RED ONION, DICED
2 GARLIC CLOVES, MINCED	1 BEEF TOMATO, DICED
1 TSP CUMIN	1 LEMON, JUICED
1 TSP TURMERIC	1 TSP WHITE WINE VINEGAR
4 TURKEY BREASTS, CUT INTO CUBES	1 TSP BLACK PEPPER
4 METAL KEBAB SKEWERS	1 TBSP OLIVE OIL
LEMON WEDGES TO GARNISH	

1. Whisk the lemon juice, garlic, cumin and turmeric in a bowl.
2. Skewer the turkey cubes using kebab sticks (metal).
3. Baste the turkey on each side with the marinade, covering for as long as possible in the fridge (don't worry if you don't have time to wait - these can be cooked straight away).
4. When ready to cook, preheat the oven to 400°F/200 °C/Gas Mark 6 and bake for 20-25 minutes or until turkey is thoroughly cooked through.
5. Prepare the salsa by mixing all the ingredients in a separate bowl.
6. Serve the turkey kebabs, garnished with the lemon wedges and the salsa on the side.

Per Serving: 193 Calories, 34G Protein, 9G Carbohydrates, 9G Fat

CARROT NOODLES & CILANTRO CHICKEN

SERVES 2 / PREP TIME: 10 MINUTES / COOK TIME: 30 MINUTES

Go easy on the carbs with this flavorsome pasta dish.

FOR THE CHICKEN:

2 SKINLESS CHICKEN BREASTS, SLICED

1 TBSP EXTRA VIRGIN OLIVE OIL

JUICE OF 1/2 LEMON

1 CLOVE GARLIC, CRUSHED

1 TBSP CILANTRO, CHOPPED

PINCH OF BLACK PEPPER

FOR THE PASTA:

5 CARROTS, PEELED

1 TSP EXTRA VIRGIN OLIVE OIL

1 TBSP SESAME SEEDS (OPTIONAL)

---

1. Pre-heat oven to 400°F/200°C/Gas Mark 6.
2. Combine 1 tbsp olive oil, lemon juice and garlic and coat the chicken slices.
3. Line a baking sheet with foil or parchment paper.
4. Layer the chicken strips and cook for 25-30 minutes or until cooked through.
5. Meanwhile, prepare your carrots by using a spiralyzer to create noodles. Alternatively use a sharp knife to cut long vertical strips from the carrot.
6. When chicken is cooked, remove from the oven and place to one side.
7. Boil a pan of water on a medium heat and add a pinch of black pepper.
8. Add your carrot to the water and boil for one minute before immediately draining.
9. Plate and serve, layering half the chicken on top and drizzling with 1 tsp olive oil , sesame seeds and cilantro.
10. Enjoy!

Per Serving: 310 Calories, 25G Protein, 5G Carbohydrates, 20G Fat

POWERFUL PESTO CHICKEN

SERVES 2 / PREP TIME: 10 MINUTES / COOK TIME: 30 MINUTES

Italian inspired chicken dish.

---

2 CHICKEN BREASTS	2 TBSP EXTRA VIRGIN OLIVE OIL
1 CUP FRESH BASIL	1/2 CUP LOW FAT HARD CHEESE (OPTIONAL)
1 CUP WATERCRESS	1 CUP BROWN RICE
1/2 CUP WALNUTS	

---

1. Preheat oven to 350°f/170°c/Gas Mark 4.
2. Add the rice to a pan of cold water over a high heat and cook for 20 minutes.
3. Meanwhile, take the chicken breasts and use a meat pounder to 'thin' each breast into a 1cm thick escalope.
4. Reserve a handful of the nuts before adding the rest of the ingredients and a little black pepper to a blender or pestle and mortar and blend until smooth.
5. Add a little water if the pesto needs loosening.
6. Coat the chicken in the pesto.
7. Bake for at least 30 minutes in the oven, or until chicken is completely cooked through.
8. Once rice has soaked up most of the water, drain and place the lid on the pan. Allow to steam.
9. Serve the chicken escalopes with the brown rice and sprinkle with the extra nuts to serve.

Per Serving: 310 Calories, 40G Protein, 25G Carbohydrates, 35G Fat

MEDITERRANEAN CHICKEN & EGGPLANT

SERVES 4 / PREP TIME: 10 MINUTES / COOK TIME: 40 MINUTES

Yummy!

4X 4OZ SKINLESS CHICKEN BREASTS OR THIGHS

1 RED ONION, CHOPPED

2 GARLIC CLOVES, CHOPPED

2 EGGPLANTS, PEELED & CHOPPED INTO CHUNKS

1 TBSP BALSAMIC VINEGAR

1 TBSP EXTRA VIRGIN OLIVE OIL

2 TBSP OREGANO, FRESH OR DRIED

2 TBSP BASIL

2 WHOLE LEMONS

1/4 CUP WATER

A PINCH OF BLACK PEPPER

---

1. Preheat the oven to 375°F/190°C/Gas Mark 5.
2. Add chicken, onion, garlic and eggplant to a lined baking tray and sprinkle over herbs and black pepper.
3. Pour over the water, olive oil and balsamic vinegar, so that the chicken and vegetables are sitting in a shallow bath.
4. Cut 1 lemon in half and add to the baking tray.
5. Bake in the oven for 35-40 minutes or until chicken is completely cooked through.
6. Serve the chicken and eggplant with a wedge of lemon each.
7. Sprinkle with freshly torn basil and black pepper to serve.
8. Enjoy with your choice of brown rice or pasta.

Per Serving: 175 Calories, 25G Protein, 3G Carbohydrates, 5G Fat

BODYBUILDING FAJITAS

SERVES 4 / PREP TIME: 15 MINUTES / COOK TIME: 45 MINUTES

A healthy version of the takeaway favorite.

---

1 ICEBERG LETTUCE

1 TSP OLIVE OIL

24 OZ GROUND LEAN TURKEY

1/2 ONION, FINELY DICED

1 RED PEPPER, FINELY DICED

1 TSP PAPRIKA

---

1. Carefully pull off the cabbage leaves from the lettuce, wash and leave intact.
2. Mix the rest of the ingredients in a bowl and divide into quarters.
3. Heat the oil in a skillet over a medium to high heat.
4. Add the turkey mixture to the pan and cook for 15-20 minutes or until cooked through.
5. Once cooked, remove from the pan and add to the centre of each lettuce leaf before wrapping fajitas style!
6. Enjoy.

Per Serving: 205 Calories, 21G Protein, 7G Carbohydrates, 17G Fat

MIGHTY STUFFED PEPPERS

SERVES 2 / PREP TIME: 5 MINUTES / COOK TIME: 40 MINUTES

This is a filling and healthy treat!

---

2 LARGE RED BELL PEPPERS, CUT IN HALF

5 OZ LEAN GROUND CHICKEN

1 CUP COOKED QUINOA

1 TBSP CAYENNE PEPPER

1 TBSP PARSLEY

1 TSP BLACK PEPPER

1/2 RED ONION, FINELY DICED

1 CLOVE GARLIC, MINCED

---

1. Preheat the oven to 350°f/170°c/Gas Mark 4.
2. Remove seeds from the middle of the bell peppers and layer onto a baking tray.
3. Combine the turkey mince with the onion, garlic, herbs, spices and quinoa.
4. Stuff the peppers with the mixture.
5. Add to the oven for 30-40 minutes or until turkey is cooked through.

Per Serving: 470 Calories, 25G Protein, 65G Carbohydrates, 11G Fat

CARIBBEAN TURKEY THIGHS

SERVES 4 / PREP TIME: 5 MINUTES / COOK TIME: 40 MINUTES

Try this homemade jerk recipe to keep you pumping!

4X TURKEY THIGHS	1 CUP BROWN RICE
1/4 CUP HONEY	1/2 CUP CANNED KIDNEY BEANS
1 TBSP MUSTARD	
2 TSP CURRY POWDER	
1 GARLIC CLOVE, MINCED	
1 TBSP JAMAICAN SPICE BLEND	
1 LIME	

---

1. Preheat the oven to 350°f/170°c/Gas Mark 4.
2. Prepare marinade by mixing butter, honey, mustard, garlic and spices and pour over the chicken.
3. Add the turkey and the marinade to a baking dish and place in oven for 35-40 minutes.
4. Meanwhile prepare your rice by bringing a pan of water to the boil, add rice and beans.
5. Cover and simmer for 20 minutes.
6. Drain and cover the rice and return to the stove for 5 minutes.
7. When turkey is cooked through, serve on a bed of rice and beans and squeeze fresh lime juice over the top.
8. Enjoy.

Per Serving: 575 Calories, 65G Protein, 24G Carbohydrates, 22G Fat

CHICKEN WITH HOMEMADE SLAW

SERVES 2 / PREP TIME: 2 MINUTES / COOK TIME: 30 MINUTES

Hit your PB with this great dish.

2 CHICKEN BREASTS	FOR THE SLAW:
1/2 LEMON, JUICED	1/2 RED CABBAGE
1 TSP BLACK PEPPER	1 CARROT
1 TSP OREGANO	1/2 LEMON, JUICED
	5 RADISHES, SLICED
	1 TBSP CILANTRO, CHOPPED

1. Preheat the broiler on a medium to high heat.
2. Cut each chicken breast in half and add to a sheet of baking paper with the pepper, lemon juice and herbs.
3. Place under the broiler for 20-25 minutes or until chicken is thoroughly cooked through. Turn once during cooking.
4. Meanwhile, prepare your slaw: Peel the carrot and grate or spiralyze.
5. Cut cabbage into very thin slices.
6. Mix all of the ingredients for the slaw in a separate bowl and toss.
7. Serve the chicken with the slaw and your choice of carbs if needed.

Per Serving: 168 Calories, 27G Protein, 4G Carbohydrates, 4G Fat

CHEEKY CHICKEN CURRY

SERVES 2 / PREP TIME: 10 MINUTES / COOK TIME: 35 MINUTES

Spicy and aromatic curry.

---

1 TBSP COCONUT OIL

1 TSP GARAM MASALA

1 TSP CUMIN

1 TSP TURMERIC

1/2 CHILI, FINELY DICED

1/2 ONION, DICED

1 CLOVE GARLIC, MINCED

1 ZUCCHINI, PEELED & SLICED

1/2 CUP CHOPPED TOMATOES, NO ADDED SALT OR SUGAR

1 CUP WATER

2 CHICKEN THIGHS/DRUMSTICKS

2 TBSP FRESH CILANTRO, FINELY CHOPPED

1 CUP BROWN RICE

1/4 CUP GREEK YOGURT

---

1. Heat oil in a pan on a medium heat and add onions, stirring for 3-4 minutes until they begin to soften.
2. Add spices one by one and stir for 4-5 minutes, releasing the flavors.
3. Now add the garlic and chili and stir.
4. Add the tomatoes and water to the pan and stir thoroughly.
5. Now add the chicken, cover and simmer for 35-40 minutes until chicken is completely cooked through.
6. Add the zucchini in the last 15 minutes.
7. Meanwhile prepare your rice by bringing a pan of water to the boil, adding rice and covering and simmering for 20 minutes.
8. Drain and cover the rice and return to the stove for 5 minutes.
9. Plate up individual rice portions and the chicken curry over the top.
10. Add a dollop of yogurt and fresh cilantro to serve.

Per Serving: 338 Calories, 32G Protein, 34G Carbohydrates, 7G Fat

LEMON CHICKEN WITH SWEDE & KALE PUREE

SERVES 2 / PREP TIME: 10 MINUTES / COOK TIME: 35 MINUTES

Lean and fresh.

2 CHICKEN BREASTS, SKINLESS	1 SWEDE
1 LEMON, JUICED	1 TSP PAPRIKA
1 TSP OREGANO	1 TSP CHILI POWDER
1 TSP BLACK PEPPER	2 METAL KEBAB STICKS
1 TSP OLIVE OIL	1 CUP KALE
	1/2 GREEN PEPPER

1. Mix the oil, lemon juice, oregano and black pepper to form a marinade.
2. Cut the chicken breasts into bite-size cubes and marinate for as long as time permits.
3. Preheat the broiler on a medium to high heat.
4. Cut the green pepper into bites-size pieces.
5. Skewer the chicken and pepper alternately.
6. Add the kebabs to a lined baking tray and broil for 20-25 minutes or until thoroughly cooked through.
7. Meanwhile, wash, peel and dice the swede into small pieces.
8. Place a pan of water on a high heat and bring to the boil.
9. Add the swede, paprika and chili powder.
10. Lower the heat and allow to cook for 20 minutes or until soft.
11. Add the kale to steam over the top for 10-15 minutes.
12. Once swede is soft and chicken is cooked, remove the chicken and place to one side.
13. Drain the swede and kale and place in a blender for 30 seconds or until puréed.
14. Add a little salt and pepper to taste here and serve with the lemon chicken kebabs.

Per Serving: 312 Calories, 27G Protein, 10G Carbohydrates, 15G Fat

TOMATO, MOZZARELLA & BASIL CHICKEN

SERVES 4 / PREP TIME: 10 MINUTES / COOK TIME: 35 MINUTES

Melt in the middle chicken thighs.

4 X BONELESS & SKINLESS CHICKEN THIGHS

1 CUP MOZZARELLA

2 BEEF TOMATOES, HALVED

4 TSP FRESH BASIL

1 TBSP BLACK PEPPER

4 COCKTAIL STICKS

1/2 CUP OLIVES, PITTED & SLICED

1 TSP OLIVE OIL

1. Preheat the oven to 350°f/170°c/Gas Mark 4.
2. Unfold the chicken thigh to fan it out flat.
3. Stuff with 1/4 mozzarella, tomato, olives and basil.
4. Fold the thigh back over and pierce through the middle with a cocktail stick.
5. Season with black pepper and drizzle with olive oil.
6. Wrap in foil or baking paper.
7. Add to a baking dish in the oven and bake for 30-35 minutes or until cooked through.
8. Serve 2 thighs each with your choice of side .

Per Serving: 300 Calories, 34G Protein, 4G Carbohydrates, 15G Fat

TURKEY & CRANBERRY SAUCE

SERVES 2 / PREP TIME: 5 MINUTES / COOK TIME: 35 MINUTES

A Christmas fave that can be enjoyed all year round!

---

2 X TURKEY BREASTS

1 CUP CRANBERRIES

1 TSP NUTMEG

1 TSP CINAMMON

1 TSP BLACK PEPPER

1 CUP WATER

1 TSP RED WINE VINEGAR

---

1. Preheat the broiler to a medium heat.
2. Butterfly the turkey breast with a sharp knife and season with a little black pepper.
3. Add to a lined baking dish and broil for 25-30 minutes or until cooked through.
4. Meanwhile, heat a pot on a medium to high heat and add the rest of the ingredients.
5. Allow to boil and then turn down the heat and simmer for 15 minutes or until reduced to a thick sauce.
6. Serve the turkey breasts once cooked with a helping of cranberry sauce and your choice of veg.

Per Serving: 200 Calories, 34G Protein, 10G Carbohydrates, 2G Fat

TANDOORI STYLE CHICKEN DRUMSTICKS

SERVES 2 / PREP TIME: 10 MINUTES / COOK TIME: 35 MINUTES

Tastes amazing with the mint dip.

---

4 X CHICKEN DRUMSTICKS, SKINLESS

1 TSP TURMERIC

1 TSP CUMIN

1 TSP GARAM MASALA

1/2 WHITE ONION, THINLY SLICED

1 GARLIC CLOVE, MINCED

1 CUP COOKED BROWN RICE

1 TSP COCONUT OIL

1 TSP CANOLA OIL

2 TBSP FRESH MINT, CHOPPED

1/2 CUP GREEK YOGURT

1/4 CUCUMBER, FINELY DICED

1 TSP CURRY POWDER

---

1. Mix the spices and garlic together with the canola oil and marinate the chicken for as long as you can.
2. Heat a large pan on a medium heat.
3. Add coconut oil until melted.
4. Add the onions for 4-5 minutes or until soft.
5. Now add the chicken drumsticks and cook for 25-30 minutes or until cooked through.
6. Meanwhile, mix the yogurt, mint, cucumber and curry powder in a small bowl and place to one side.
7. Serve with brown rice and a helping of the mint dip.

Per Serving: 625 Calories, 51G Protein, 37G Carbohydrates, 29g Fat

TURKEY MEATBALLS & COUSCOUS

SERVES 2 / PREP TIME: 2 MINUTES / COOK TIME: 30 MINUTES

Juicy meatballs served with a herby side.

10 OZ GROUND TURKEY	1 CUP COUSCOUS
1 EGG WHITE	1 TBSP OLIVE OIL
1/4 CUP CANNED TOMATOES	1 TBSP CRUSHED ALMONDS
1/2 LEMON, JUICED	1 TSP BALSAMIC VINEGAR
1 TSP BLACK PEPPER	1/2 ONION, DICED
2 TBSP FRESH PARSLEY, CHOPPED	1 GARLIC CLOVE, MINCED

1. Mix the ground turkey with the egg white, black pepper, balsamic vinegar and 1 tbsp parsley.
2. Use your hands to shape into meatballs.
3. Heat the oil in a skillet over a medium to high heat.
4. Add the onions and garlic and saute until soft (4-5 minutes).
5. Now add the meatballs and brown each side.
6. Add the chopped tomatoes and allow to cook for 15-20 minutes or until meat is thoroughly cooked through.
7. Meanwhile, add the couscous to a bowl and pour over boiling water to just cover the couscous.
8. Cover and allow to steam for 5 minutes.
9. Now add 1 tbsp parsley, lemon juice and crushed nuts.
10. Serve the meatballs (the sauce should be reduced to a thick sauce by now) over the couscous.

Per Serving: 460 Calories, 35G Protein, 35G Carbohydrates, 21g Fat

MEAT

ROASTED RUMP & ROOT VEG

SERVES 2 / PREP TIME: 10 MINUTES / COOK TIME: 7 HOURS IN CROCK POT

Rich in iron and B vitamins - steak is a staple in the body building world.

16 OZ OF LEAN RUMP STEAK

1 TBSP THYME

1 TSP FRENCH MUSTARD

1 TBSP OLIVE OIL

1 TSP PEPPER

1 ONION CUT, PEELED AND SLICED

1 PARSNIP, PEELED AND DICED

1 RUTABAGA, PEELED AND SLICED

2 GARLIC CLOVES

1. Preheat the oven to 450°f/250°c/Gas Mark 8.
2. Meanwhile, mix the herbs and black pepper with the mustard and olive oil.
3. Coat the rump steak and allow to marinate for as long as possible.
4. Add the rump steak to a shallow oven dish and heat the hob to a high heat. Sear each side of the beef steak for a few minutes until browned. If the baking dish is not suitable to place on the hob do this in a separate skillet first.
5. Now add the vegetables and whole garlic cloves (skin on) to the baking dish (if your beef is already in the dish make sure you use tongs to lift it first).
6. Add the dish to the oven for 25 minutes before turning the heat down to 300°f/150°c/Gas Mark 2.
7. Continue to cook for a further 8 minutes and then remove and allow to rest (the beef will continue to cook in the resting time).
8. After 5 minutes, slice the steak with a carving knife and serve on top of the juicy vegetables. The garlic should be deliciously soft by now so serve this up too!
9. Enjoy.

Per Serving: 558 Calories, 62G Protein, 22G Carbohydrates, 21g Fat

MIX 'N' MATCH BEEF BURGER

SERVES 2 / PREP TIME: 5 MINUTES / COOK TIME: 25 MINUTES

Mix up the toppings to create your favorite burgers at home.

---

8 OZ OF LEAN 100% GRASS-FED GROUND BEEF

1 EGG WHITE

1 TSP BLACK PEPPER

1 TSP PAPRIKA

1 TSP MUSTARD

2 MINI GHERKINS, SLICED

1 BEEF TOMATO, SLICED

1/4 CUP ARUGULA

2 WHOLEGRAIN BUNS

---

1. Preheat the broiler to a medium high heat.
2. Mix the ground beef with the herbs, egg white, spices and mustard.
3. Use your hands to form 2 patties (about 1 inch thick).
4. Add to an oven proof baking dish and broil for 15 minutes or until meat is thoroughly cooked through. Use a knife to insert into the centre - the juices should run clear.
5. Slice your burger buns and stack with the burger, gherkin, tomato and arugula.
6. Add a little extra mustard to taste.

Per Serving: 411 Calories, 32G Protein, 37G Carbohydrates, 12g Fat

FIT LAMB STEAKS WITH TZATZIKI

SERVES 2 / PREP TIME: 5 MINUTES / COOK TIME: 20 MINUTES

Lean lamb can still be enjoyed as a treat!

---

2 X 5OZ LEAN LAMB STEAKS

1 TBSP FRESH ROSEMARY, FINELY CHOPPED

1 TBSP EXTRA VIRGIN OLIVE OIL

1 LEMON, JUICED

1 TSP WHITE WINE VINEGAR

1/2 CUP OF LOW FAT GREEK YOGURT

1/4 CUCUMBER, CHOPPED

1/4 CUP FRESH MINT

1/2 CUP SPINACH

1 CUP COUSCOUS

1/2 RED ONION, FINELY DICED

---

1. Mix the olive oil with the rosemary and marinate the lamb steaks for as long as possible.
2. Heat a skillet over a medium to high heat and add the marinated steaks, cooking for 10 minutes on each side or until thoroughly cooked through.
3. Meanwhile, add the couscous to a heatproof bowl, pour boiling water over the top, cover and leave to steam for 5 minutes.
4. Stir through the diced red pepper and 1/2 lemon juice.
5. Mix the yogurt, 1/2 lemon juice, vinegar, mint and cucumber for your tzatziki. Season with a little salt and pepper.
6. Serve the lamb steaks with the couscous and tzatziki on the side.

Per Serving: 403 Calories, 40G Protein, 25G Carbohydrates, 15g Fat

BODYBUILDING BEEF STEW

SERVES 2 / PREP TIME: 10 MINUTES / COOK TIME OVERNIGHT

Stick this in the slow cooker for succulent and tender meat.

1 TBSP OF EXTRA VIRGIN OLIVE OIL

8 OZ LEAN BEEF, CUBED

1 ONION, DICED

4 CUPS OF WATER

1 TSP CUMIN

1 TSP TURMERIC

1 TSP CURRY POWDER

1 TSP OREGANO

2 SWEET POTATOES, PEELED AND CUBED

1 RED BELL PEPPER, ROUGHLY CHOPPED

1 BAY LEAF

1. Heat the olive oil in a skillet over a medium to high heat.
2. Add the beef and cook for 5 minutes or until browned on each side.
3. Add the vegetables and garlic to the slow cooker and pour in the water.
4. Now add the herbs, spices and bay leaf.
5. Then cover the slow cooker and cook for at least 8 hours or overnight.
6. Plate up and serve when ready to eat!

Per Serving: 372 Calories, 25G Protein, 42G Carbohydrates, 12g Fat

MUSCLE MEATBALL & CELERIAC SPAGHETTI

SERVES 2 / PREP TIME: 5 MINUTES / COOK TIME: 20 MINUTES

Mega meaty dish with a fresh pasta.

---

8 OZ LEAN PORK/BEEF MINCE

1 GARLIC CLOVE, CRUSHED

1 TSP DRIED THYME

2 TBSP EXTRA VIRGIN OLIVE OIL

1/2 RED ONION, FINELY CHOPPED

1 CELERIAC

FOR THE SAUCE:

1 TBSP EXTRA VIRGIN OLIVE OIL

1 CUP FRESH TOMATOES, CHOPPED (SEEDS & JUICES SAVED)

1/4 CUP FRESH PARSLEY

---

1. Mix the mince, 1 tbsp oil, garlic, onion and herbs in a bowl. Season with a little black pepper and separate into 8 balls, rolling with the palms of your hands.
2. Heat 1 tbsp oil in a pan over a medium heat and add the meatballs for 5 minutes or until browned.
3. Add the tomatoes, parsley (save some for garnishing) and extra olive oil.
4. Cover and lower heat to simmer for 15 minutes.
5. Meanwhile, prepare the celeriac by carefully removing any nobbly bits from the skin with a sharp knife. Use a spiralyzer to create spaghetti strips with the celeriac (place it in lengthways). If you don't have a spiralyzer you can use a potato peeler once you've cut the celeriac into quarters.
6. Add a pot of water to boil over a high heat and add the celeriac spaghetti over a steamer for 5-10 minutes or until slightly soft.
7. Drain celeriac, portion up and add meatballs and sauce over the top to serve.
8. Sprinkle with a little freshly torn basil!

Per Serving: 374 Calories, 30G Protein, 35G Carbohydrates, 26g Fat

Lemongrass & Chili Beef

SERVES 2 /   PREP TIME: 5 MINUTES / COOK TIME: 20 MINUTES

Fresh and filling.

---

1 TBSP COCONUT OIL

2X 6OZ LEAN FRYING STEAK, CUT INTO STRIPS

1 STICK LEMONGRASS,

1 TSP CHILI FLAKES

1/2 CUP SUGAR SNAP PEAS/GREEN BEANS

1/2 GREEN PEPPER, SLICED

1 GARLIC CLOVE, MINCED

1 TBSP HONEY

1 CUP BROWN RICE

1/4 CUP GREEN ONIONS, CHOPPED

1 LEMON, JUICED

---

1. Into a blender or pestle and mortar, add the oil, lemongrass, chili flakes, garlic and honey and blitz until nearly smooth.
2. Marinate the beef for as long as possible.
1. Heat the oil in a skillet or wok over a medium to high heat.
2. Add the beef strips and brown each side for 4 minutes.
3. Now add the green pepper and continue to cook for a further 10 minutes.
4. Add the green onions and sugar snap peas for a few more minutes.
5. Plate up and serve with brown rice and lime juice over the top.

Per Serving: 289 Calories, 21G Protein, 32G Carbohydrates, 8g Fat

POWERFUL PORK & SPEEDY SAUERKRAUT

SERVES 2 /   PREP TIME: 5 MINUTES /   COOK TIME: 20 MINUTES

A German inspired meal with heaps of vitamins.

2X 4OZ LEAN PORK LOINS

1/2 WHITE CABBAGE, SLICED

1 TSP SALT

1 TBSP WHITE WINE VINEGAR

2 CARROTS, PEELED AND SLICED

1 TSP NUTMEG

---

1. Preheat the broiler to a medium high heat.
2. Sprinkle pork with nutmeg.
3. Add the pork loins to a baking tray and place under the broiler for 10-15 minutes or according to package guidelines.
4. Meanwhile, place a pot of water over a medium to high heat and add the cabbage and carrots for 5-10 minutes or until slightly softer.
5. Add the salt and vinegar to the pan.
6. Drain the cabbage and carrots and serve with the pork.
7. Enjoy!

Per Serving: 179 Calories, 25G Protein, 17G Carbohydrates, 5g Fat

MUSCLE-FRIENDLY LASAGNE

SERVES 2 / PREP TIME: 10 MINUTES / COOK TIME: 50 MINUTES

Delicious & filling muscle building recipe

---

10 OZ LEAN GROUND BEEF

1 GARLIC CLOVE, MINCED

1 ONION, DICED

1 TSP CAYENNE PEPPER

1 TSP PARSLEY

1/2 CUP CANNED TOMATOES

1 TSP BLACK PEPPER

2 EGGPLANTS, SLICED VERTICALLY

FOR THE WHITE SAUCE:

1/4 CUP ALL PURPOSE WHITE FLOUR

3/4 CUP RICE MILK

1 TBSP GHEE

1/4 TEASPOON WHITE PEPPER

1 TSP BLACK PEPPER

---

1. Preheat the oven to 350°f/170°c/Gas Mark 4.
2. To prepare the beef: Heat oil in a skillet on a medium to high heat and add onions and garlic for 5 minutes until soft.
3. Add lean beef mince, season with herbs and spices, add water and cook for 10-15 minutes or until completely browned.
4. Meanwhile prepare white sauce:
5. Heat saucepan on a medium heat.
6. Add the butter to the pan on the side nearest to the handle.
7. Tilt the pan towards you and allow butter to melt, whilst trying not to let it cover the rest of the pan.
8. Now add the flour to the opposite side of the pan and gradually mix the flour into the butter - continue to mix until smooth.
9. Add the milk and mix thoroughly for 10 minutes until lumps dissolve.
10. Add pepper.
11. Turn off the heat and place to one side.
12. Layer an oven proof lasagne dish with 1/3 eggplant slices.
13. Add 1/3 beef mince on top.
14. Layer with 1/3 white sauce.
15. Repeat until ingredients are used.
16. Cover and add to the oven for 25-30 minutes or until golden and bubbly.
17. Remove and serve piping hot!

Per Serving: 369 Calories, 31G Protein, 40G Carbohydrates, 9g Fat

BARBELL BEEF CURRY

SERVES 2 / PREP TIME: 10 MINUTES / COOK TIME: 1 HOUR

Scrumptious beef dish.

---

1 TSP OLIVE OIL

10 OZ LEAN FRYING BEEF, CUT INTO STRIPS

1 ONION, DICED

1 GARLIC CLOVE, MINCED

1 SWEET POTATO, PEELED & ROUGHLY CHOPPED

1 TBSP CURRY POWDER

1 CUP ALMOND OR RICE MILK

1 TBSP CILANTRO

---

1. Heat oil in a pot over a medium to high heat and sauté onions and garlic for 5 minutes or until soft.
2. Add the beef for 5-10 minutes, turning to brown each side, before adding the milk and curry powder.
3. Bring to the boil, then turn down the heat and add the sweet potato to the curry.
4. Cover and simmer for 45-50 minutes or until the beef is soft.
5. Scatter with cilantro and serve with rice.
6. Top tip: you could transfer the curry to a slow cooker and leave overnight to free you up from the stove if you wish - just ensure the liquid covers the ingredients.

Per Serving: 418 Calories, 32G Protein, 32G Carbohydrates, 18g Fat

CHILI BEEF & MANGO SALSA

SERVES 2 / PREP TIME: 10 MINUTES / COOK TIME: 35 MINUTES

Spice things up in the kitchen.

1 RED ONION, DICED	2 TBSP EXTRA VIRGIN OLIVE OIL
1/2 RED BELL PEPPER, DICED	1/2 CUP CHERRY TOMATOES, DICED
1 GARLIC CLOVE, MINCED	1/4 CUP MANGO, DICED
10 OZ LEAN GROUND BEEF	1/2 LIME, JUICED
1 RED CHILI, FINELY DICED	1 CUP QUINOA
1/4 CUP KIDNEY BEANS	1 TBSP FRESH CILANTRO

1. Bring a pan of water to the boil and add quinoa for 20 minutes.
2. Meanwhile, add 1 tbsp oil to a pan and heat on a medium to high heat.
3. Add the half the onions, pepper, chili and garlic and sauté for 5 minutes until soft.
4. Add the beef to the pan and stir until browned.
5. Now add the kidney beans and the water, cover and turn the heat down a little to simmer for 20 minutes.
6. Meanwhile, drain the water from the quinoa, add the lid and steam while the chili is cooking.
7. Prepare the salsa by mixing the rest of the onion, tomatoes, lime juice, cilantro and mango.
8. Serve chili hot with the quinoa and salsa.

Per Serving: 591 Calories, 39G Protein, 51G Carbohydrates, 27g Fat

CHUNKY CHINESE STIR FRY

SERVES 2 / PREP TIME: 10 MINUTES / COOK TIME: 1 HOUR

Easy to prepare and tastes delicious.

---

1 TSP COCONUT OIL	1 TBSP GINGER, MINCED
10 OZ LEAN FRYING BEEF, CUT INTO STRIPS	1 TSP CHINESE 5 SPICE
1/2 CUP GREEN ONIONS, DICED	1/4 CUP WATER CHESTNUTS
1 GARLIC CLOVE, MINCED	1/2 CUP BROCCOLI FLORETS
1 CUP WHOLE-WHEAT NOODLES	1 CUP COCONUT MILK

---

1. Heat oil in a wok over a high heat and sauté the beef for 5-10 minutes, turning to brown each side.
2. Add the garlic and ginger to the pan and sauté for a few minutes.
3. Now add the coconut milk, spices and water chestnuts and allow to simmer on a medium heat for 25-35 minutes or until beef is soft.
4. Meanwhile prepare noodles according to package guidelines.
5. Add the broccoli and green onions 10 minutes before serving.
6. Serve the beef over the noodles and enjoy.

Per Serving: 433 Calories, 33G Protein, 26G Carbohydrates, 21g Fat

MOROCCAN LAMB TAGINE

SERVES 2 / PREP TIME: 5 MINUTES / COOK TIME: 1 HOUR & 15 MINUTES

Hearty, wholesome and super easy to make!

---

1 TBSP OF OLIVE OIL

2 LEAN LAMB FILLETS, CUBED

1 ONION, CHOPPED

2 CARROTS, CUBED

1/2 CUP SPINACH

4 CUPS OF HOMEMADE CHICKEN STOCK

1 TSP DRIED ROSEMARY

1 TSP OF CHOPPED PARSLEY

1/2 CUP RAISINS

4 TBSP FLAKED ALMONDS

---

1. In a large casserole dish, heat the olive oil on a medium high heat.
2. Add the lamb and cook for 5 minutes until browned.
3. Add the chopped onion and carrots. Leave to cook for another 5 minutes until the vegetables begin to soften.
4. Add the chicken stock, spinach, raisins and rosemary.
5. Then cover the casserole and leave to simmer on a low heat for 1-1.5 hours until the lamb is tender and fully cooked through.
6. Plate up and serve with the chopped parsley and flaked almonds to garnish.

Per Serving: 380 Calories, 34G Protein, 12G Carbohydrates, 25g Fat

LEAN BEEF STROGANOFF

SERVES 2 / PREP TIME: 10 MINUTES / COOK TIME: 4-5 HOURS

Healthy and filling.

1/2 ONION, DICED

1 GARLIC CLOVE, MINCED

6 OZ LEAN FRYING BEEF

1 CUP LOW SALT CHICKEN OR VEGETABLE STOCK

1 TSP DRIED OREGANO

1 TBSP BLACK PEPPER

1/2 CUP LOW FAT CREME FRAICHE

1/4 CUP WHOLE WHEAT FLOUR

2 TBSP WATER

1 CUP BROWN RICE

---

1. In a crockpot or slow cooker, add the pepper, oregano, garlic, onion, stock and beef.
2. Cover and cook on high for 4-5 hours or until beef is tender.
3. Add the water, flour and creme fraiche to the crock pot and mix until smooth.
4. Continue to cook for another 20 minutes or until the mixture has thickened.
5. Meanwhile, bring a pan of water to the boil and add the rice for 20 minutes.
6. Drain the water from the rice, add the lid and steam for 5 minutes.
7. Serve the rice with the creamy beef over the top and enjoy!

Per Serving: 382 Calories, 32G Protein, 44G Carbohydrates, 12g Fat

CHILI BEEF IN LETTUCE TORTILLAS

SERVES 2 / PREP TIME: 10 MINUTES / COOK TIME: 30 MINUTES

These delicious wraps are great for lunch or dinner and are loved by the whole family!

---

1 GARLIC CLOVE, MINCED

1/2 CUCUMBER, DICED

8 OZ LEAN GROUND BEEF

1 TBSP CHILI FLAKES

4 ICEBERG LETTUCE LEAVES, WASHED

1 TSP OLIVE OIL

---

1. Mix the ground meat with the garlic and chili flakes.
2. Heat oil in a skillet over a medium heat.
3. Add the beef to the pan and cook for 20-25 minutes or until cooked through.
4. Serve beef mixture with diced cucumber in each lettuce wrap and fold.

Per Serving: 141 Calories, 22G Protein, 2G Carbohydrates, 3g Fat

BEEF & PEARL BARLEY CASSEROLE

SERVES 4 / PREP TIME: 5 MINUTES / COOK TIME: 40 MINUTES

Absolutely delicious

---

2 CUPS PEARL BARLEY

12OZ LEAN CASSEROLE BEEF, CUBED

1 CUP CHICKEN/BEEF/VEG STOCK

1 CARROT, PEELED & CHOPPED

1 CELERY STALK, CHOPPED

1 BAY LEAF

1 TBSP PAPRIKA

1 TSP PEPPER

1 TSP THYME

1 CUP WHITE CABBAGE, SHREDDED

1 TBSP OLIVE OIL

---

1. Heat the oil in a large pot over a medium to high heat and add the beef.
2. Brown each side, cooking for 6-7 minutes.
3. Now add the stock and 1 cup water along with all the rest of the ingredients.
4. Turn the heat down to a medium heat and allow to cook slowly for 1-2 hours.
(Alternatively you can transfer the beef and the rest of the ingredients to a slow cooker and leave to cook overnight.)
5. Serve hot and enjoy!

Per Serving: 531 Calories, 28G Protein, 81G Carbohydrates, 8g Fat

EGGPLANT & SWEET POTATO LASAGNE

SERVES 2 / PREP TIME: 10 MINUTES / COOK TIME: 50 MINUTES

Inspired by the Greek recipe but made for body builders!

---

1 GARLIC CLOVE, MINCED

1 ONION, DICED

8 OZ LEAN GROUND BEEF

1 TSP CAYENNE PEPPER

1 TSP THYME

1/2 CUP WATER

1 TSP BLACK PEPPER

1 EGGPLANT, SLICED

1 SWEET POTATO, PEELED & SLICED

1 CUP CANNED TOMATOES

FOR THE CHEESE SAUCE:

1/4 CUP COTTAGE CHEESE

3/4 CUP RICE MILK

1/4 TEASPOON WHITE PEPPER

1 TSP BLACK PEPPER

---

1. Preheat the oven to 350°f/170°c/Gas Mark 4.
2. To prepare cheese sauce: Whisk the cottage cheese into the rice milk until smooth. Season with the pepper and place to one side.
3. Heat oil in a skillet on a medium to high heat and add onions and garlic for 5 minutes until soft.
4. Add lean beef mince, season with herbs and spices, add tomatoes and water and cook for 10-15 minutes or until completely browned.
5. Layer an oven proof lasagne dish with 1/3 eggplant slices.
6. Add 1/3 beef mince on top.
7. Add 1/3 sweet potato slices on top.
8. Layer with 1/3 cheese sauce.
9. Repeat until ingredients are used.
10. Cover and add to the oven for 25-30 minutes or until golden and bubbly.
11. Remove and serve piping hot!

Per Serving: 340 Calories, 30G Protein, 42G Carbohydrates, 7g Fat

STEAK, EGG & MUSHROOM FRENZY

SERVES 2 / PREP TIME: 10 MINUTES / COOK TIME: 20 MINUTES

A classic!

2X 8OZ RUMP STEAK, SLICED

4 EGGS

2 PORTABELLO MUSHROOMS, SLICED

1 BEEF TOMATO, SLICED IN HALF

1 GARLIC CLOVE, MINCED

1 TSP PEPPERCORNS, CRUSHED

1 TSP CHILI POWDER

1/4 CUP GREEN ONIONS, CHOPPED

1 TBSP OLIVE OIL

---

1. Mix the olive oil, chili powder and peppercorns in a shallow dish and marinade the steak for as long as possible.
2. Heat a dry skillet over a high heat.
3. When extremely hot, add the steak slices and allow to cook for 65minutes before turning over (try not to move it around the pan at all in this time).
4. Add the sliced mushroom, tomato and garlic to the pan and allow all the ingredients to sauté for a further 4 minutes.
5. Whisk the eggs with the green onions and pour over the ingredients.
6. Allow to cook like you would an omelette for 4-5 minutes or until eggs are cooked through.
7. Slide out of the skillet with a spatula.
8. Cut into 2 portions and serve.

Per Serving: 383 Calories, 44G Protein, 10G Carbohydrates, 17g Fat

RED THAI CURRY WITH DUCK

SERVES 2 / PREP TIME: 10 MINUTES / COOK TIME: 50 MINUTES

Delicious and fresh curry with an added sweet surprise.

---

2 X DUCK BREASTS, SKINLESS

1/2 WHITE ONION, DICED

1 RED CHILI, DICED

1 RED BELL PEPPER, DICED

2 TBSP FRESH BASIL LEAVES

1/2 STICK LEMON GRASS, CHOPPED

1/2 CUP COCONUT MILK

1/2 CUP CHICKEN STOCK

1 CUP COOKED BROWN RICE

1 TBSP COCONUT OIL

1 GARLIC CLOVE, MINCED

---

1. Blend the chili, red pepper, basil, lemon grass and oil in a blender until a paste is formed. Alternatively use a pestle and mortar.
2. Heat a wok or skillet over a medium to high heat.
3. Spray a little cooking spray into the pan and add the duck breasts for 4 minutes on each side or until brown.
4. Add the onions and garlic and sauté for 3 minutes.
5. Now pour the coconut milk, stock and paste into the pan and stir until it dissolves.
6. Allow to simmer on a medium to low heat for 30-40 minutes or until duck is soft.
7. Add the pineapple pieces and green beans 7 minutes before serving
8. Serve with the brown rice.

Per Serving: 373 Calories, 32G Protein, 31G Carbohydrates, 15g Fat

SLOW COOKED SPICY STEAK & BEANS

SERVES 2 / PREP TIME: 10 MINUTES / COOK TIME: OVERNIGHT

An easy dish to prepare in your slow cooker.

16 OZ BEEF STEAK, DICED

1/2 WHITE ONION, DICED

1 RED BELL PEPPER, DICED

1 CARROT, PEELED & SLICED

1 CUP CANNED TOMATOES

1/2 CUP CHICKEN STOCK

2 CUP COOKED BROWN RICE

1 GARLIC CLOVE, MINCED

1/2 CUP BLACK BEANS, CANNED

1 TSP OREGANO

1 TSP THYME

1 TSP BLACK PEPPER

1 TBSP OLIVE OIL

1 TSP CURRY POWDER

1. Mix the olive oil with the herbs and marinade the steak for as long as possible.
2. Add to a slow cooker with the rest of the ingredients and cook overnight.
3. Serve with brown rice for a hearty meal.

Per Serving: 394 Calories, 40G Protein, 37G Carbohydrates, 10g Fat

SWEET POTATO COTTAGE PIE

SERVES 2 / PREP TIME: 10 MINUTES / COOK TIME: 1 HOUR

A twist on the British classic.

---

10 OZ LEAN GROUND BEEF

1 ONION, DICED

3 SWEET POTATOES, PEELED & SLICED

1 TBSP GREEK YOGURT

1 CARROT, PEELED & DICED

1 TSP BLACK PEPPER

1/2 RED BELL PEPPER, DICED

1 CUP MUSHROOMS, SLICED

1 TSP OLIVE OIL

1/2 CUP WATER

1 TSP THYME

---

1. Preheat the oven to 350°f/170°c/Gas Mark 4.
2. Bring a pot of water to the boil and add the sweet potatoes.
3. Turn down the heat slightly and allow to simmer for 30 minutes.
4. Meanwhile, add oil to a pan on a medium heat.
5. Add the onions and sauté for 4-5 minutes or until soft.
6. Now add the carrots and red pepper and sauté for a further 5 minutes.
7. Add the ground beef and mix until beef is browned.
8. Add the water, turn the heat to high until it starts to bubble and then reduce the heat and add the thyme and black pepper.
9. Remove from the heat and check that the sweet potatoes are soft with a fork.
10. Drain and mash with a potato masher, adding the Greek yogurt.
11. Pour the beef mixture into a rectangular oven dish.
12. Top with the sweet potato mash.
13. Use your fork to gently score the top of the mash potato, creating soft lines along the top.
14. Add to the oven for 30-40 minutes or until golden brown.
15. Remove and serve with your choice of greens on the side.

Per Serving: 421 Calories, 33G Protein, 45G Carbohydrates, 13g Fat

BEEF CHILI CON CARNE

SERVES 2 / PREP TIME: 10 MINUTES / COOK TIME: 30 MINUTES

A winter warmer!

---

10 OZ LEAN GROUND BEEF	1 TBSP CHILI POWDER
1 ONION, DICED	1 GARLIC CLOVE, MINCED
1/2 CUP KIDNEY BEANS	1 TSP CILANTRO
1 CARROT, PEELED & DICED	1 LIME
1/2 RED BELL PEPPER, DICED	1 CUP COOKED WILD RICE/QUINOA
1 CUP MUSHROOMS, SLICED	
1 TSP OLIVE OIL	
1/2 CUP WATER	

---

1. Heat the oil in a large pot over a medium to high heat.
2. Add the onions and garlic and sauté for 5-6 minutes or until soft.
3. Add the carrot and cook for a further 5 minutes.
4. Sprinkle with chili powder.
5. Add the ground beef to the pan and stir until browned.
6. Now add the kidney beans, water and herbs.
7. Leave to cook on a medium heat for 20 minutes or until beef thoroughly cooked through.
8. Serve with a squeeze of lime juice and your choice of rice or quinoa.

Per Serving: 665 Calories, 43G Protein, 85G Carbohydrates, 18g Fat

VEGETARIAN & VEGAN

TRAINING TOFU BROTH

SERVES 2 / PREP TIME: 5 MINUTES / COOK TIME: 15 MINUTES

Tofu is a protein source and soaks up all the flavors it's cooked in.

1 PACK OF DRAINED, PRESSED AND CUBED TOFU

1 TBSP COCONUT OIL

1/2 ONION, SLICED

1 CUP UDON NOODLES/BROWN RICE,

1 CUP OF SUGAR SNAP PEAS

1/2 CHILI, FINELY SLICED

1/2 CUP COCONUT MILK

1/2 CUP (HOMEMADE) VEG STOCK

1 BOK CHOY

1 TBSP LIME JUICE

1/2 CUP WATER CHESTNUTS

1/4 CUP GREEN ONIONS, SLICED

1. Heat the oil in a wok on a high heat and then sauté the tofu until brown on each side.
2. Add the onion and sauté for 2-3 minutes.
3. Add the coconut milk and stock to the wok until it starts to bubble.
4. Lower to a medium heat and add the noodles, chili and water chestnuts.
5. Allow to simmer for 10-15 minutes and then add the bok choy and sugar snap peas for 5 minutes.
6. Serve with a sprinkle of green onions.

Per Serving: 517 Calories, 24G Protein, 67G Carbohydrates, 31g Fat

MEXICAN BEANS & QUINOA

SERVES 4 / PREP TIME: 5 MINUTES / COOK TIME: 20 MINUTES

Beans are a great source of vitamins and fibre as well as protein. These taste amazing.

---

1 TBSP OLIVE OIL

1 CUP OF QUINOA

1 ONION, DICED

1 GARLIC CLOVE, DICED

1 TSP OREGANO

1 TSP PARSLEY

1/2 CUP BLACK BEANS

1/2 CUP KIDNEY BEANS

1/4 CUP RED LENTILS, SOAKED

1 AVOCADO, SLICED

2 TBSP OF PLAIN NON-FAT GREEK YOGURT

1 TSP PAPRIKA

1 TSP CHILI FLAKES

1 TBSP FRESH CILANTRO

1 LEMON, JUICED

---

1. Heat a pan of water on a high heat and add quinoa, allowing to cook for 15 minutes.
2. In a separate pan heat the oil over a medium heat and add the onions and garlic to sauté for 3-4 minutes.
3. Now add the beans and lentils as well as the oregano and parsley and stir through.
4. Add 1 cup of water and allow the beans to simmer for 20-25 minutes or until soft.
5. Meanwhile, in a separate bowl, crush the avocado into the yogurt with a fork and squeeze in a little lemon juice. Sprinkle with paprika.
6. Once quinoa has soaked up most of the liquid, add the rest of the lemon juice and a little salt and pepper.
7. Serve with the beans (the liquid should have been absorbed and the beans and lentils soft) and the avocado dip.
8. Enjoy!

Per Serving: 329 Calories, 12G Protein, 50G Carbohydrates, 13g Fat

VEGAN LASAGNE

SERVES 2 / PREP TIME: 10 MINUTES / COOK TIME: 1 HOUR

Creamy, bubbling lasagne!

1/2 PACK OF SOFT TOFU

1 CUP OF ALMOND MILK

1 RED ONION, DICED

1 GARLIC CLOVE, MINCED

1 TSP OREGANO

1 TSP BASIL

1 CAN OF CHOPPED TOMATOES

A PINCH OF BLACK PEPPER TO TASTE

1 ZUCCHINI , SLICED

1 RED PEPPER, SLICED

1 EGGPLANT, SLICED

1 TBSP OLIVE OIL

---

1. Preheat oven to 325°F/170 °C/Gas Mark 3.
2. Slice zucchini, eggplant and pepper into vertical strips (think lasagne sheets).
3. Add the almond milk and tofu to a food processor and blitz until smooth. Place to one side.
4. Heat the oil in a skillet over a medium heat and add the onions and garlic for 3-4 minutes or until soft.
5. Now add the canned tomatoes, herbs and pepper and allow to stir through for 5-6 minutes until hot.
6. Into a lasagne or suitable oven dish, layer 1/3 the eggplant, followed by 1/3 zucchini, then 1/3 pepper before pouring over 1/3 of the tomato sauce and 1/3 tofu white sauce.
7. Repeat for the next 2 layers, finishing with the white sauce.
8. Add to the oven for 40-50 minutes or until veg is soft and can easily by sliced into servings.

Per Serving: 301 Calories, 18G Protein, 15G Carbohydrates, 15g Fat

TOASTED SESAME & PEANUT TOFU

SERVES 2 / PREP TIME: 5 MINUTES / COOK TIME: 15 MINUTES

Aromatic & energizing!

---

1 PACK FIRM TOFU, PRESSED & CUBED

1/4 CUP SESAME SEEDS

1 TBSP SMOOTH WHOLE PEANUT BUTTER

1 TBSP ALMOND OR RICE MILK

1 CUP TENDERSTEM BROCCOLI/GREEN BEANS

1/2 LIME, JUICED

1 TBSP COCONUT OIL

---

1. Add the peanut butter to the milk and whisk until loosened and add to a shallow bowl.
2. Add sesame seeds to a shallow bowl.
3. Once the tofu has been pressed for as long as possible (to get rid of extra liquid), dip each cube into the peanut milk to cover and then dip straight into the sesame seeds to coat. If they don't cover perfectly don't worry!
4. Heat the oil in a wok or skillet over a high heat.
5. Once hot, add the tofu to the pan and pour in any extra peanut milk and seeds.
6. Allow to cook for 10-15 minutes, occasionally turning to brown each side.
7. Meanwhile, boil a pan of water and add the broccoli/green beans and cook to package guidelines.
8. Serve the tofu on a bed of greens and enjoy.

Per Serving: 370 Calories, 21G Protein, 9G Carbohydrates, 25g Fat

HALLOUMI BURGERS & CHILI KETCHUP

SERVES 2 / PREP TIME: 2 MINUTES / COOK TIME: 20 MINUTES

Possibly better than a beef burger!

---

4 SLICES HALLOUMI CHEESE

2 WHOLEGRAIN PITTA BREADS

1/4 CUP ARUGULA

1/2 CUP BUTTON MUSHROOMS, DICED

1 RED CHILI, FINELY DICED

1 CUP TOMATOES

1 TSP STEVIA

1 TBSP OLIVE OIL

1 RED ONION, DICED

---

1. Prepare the chili ketchup by heating the oil in a skillet over a medium heat. Add the onions and sweat for 3-4 minutes.
2. Now add the fresh tomatoes, mushrooms and chili and turn down the heat.
3. Leave to simmer whilst preparing the burgers - add a tbsp water to stop it sticking.
4. Meanwhile, heat a griddle pan or broiler on a medium to high heat and add the halloumi slices for 5-10 minutes.
5. Lightly toast the pitta breads.
6. Place the tomato mixture (which should be nice and thick by now) into a food processor and blend until smooth. If you don't have one don't worry - the ketchup is still great chunky
7. Serve the halloumi in the pitta with the arugula and chili ketchup.

Per Serving: 417 Calories, 19G Protein, 22G Carbohydrates, 19g Fat

STRONG SPAGHETTI SQUASH QUINOA

SERVES 2 / PREP TIME: 15 MINUTES / COOK TIME: 50 MINUTES

A hearty dish to build strength.

---

1 SPAGHETTI SQUASH, HALVED AND DE-SEEDED

1 TBSP OF EXTRA VIRGIN OLIVE OIL

1/2 CUP QUINOA

1 TSP ROSEMARY, CHOPPED

1 TSP TARRAGON

1 TSP BLACK PEPPER

---

1. Pre-heat the oven to 375°F/190 °C/Gas Mark 5.
2. Grab a large baking dish and arrange the squash halves with the cut side down and pour half a cup of water into the dish.
3. Bake for around 45 minutes or until tender and remove the dish from the oven. Turn the squash over and allow to slightly cool.
4. Meanwhile, heat a pan of water on a medium to high heat and add oil and quinoa as well as the herbs. Bring to a boil and then turn down the heat and allow to simmer for 15 minutes.
5. Once the quinoa has soaked up most of the liquid, place the lid on the pan and allow to steam.
6. Use a fork to scrape the flesh from the spaghetti squash and then dice.
7. Stir through the quinoa and add a little black pepper and extra oil to serve if desired.

Per Serving: 400 Calories, 12G Protein, 63G Carbohydrates, 11g Fat

SPICED CAULIFLOWER & CHICKPEA CURRY

SERVES 2 / PREP TIME: 5 MINUTES / COOK TIME: 35 MINUTES

This dish is full of flavor and texture and the protein from the chickpeas adds up!

1 CAULIFLOWER, FLORETS

2 CUP CHICKPEAS (CANNED OR SOAKED)

1 ONION, DICED

1 GARLIC CLOVE, MINCED

1 TSP CUMIN

1 TSP TURMERIC

1 TSP GARAM MASALA

1/2 CHILI, DICED

1 TBSP COCONUT OIL

1 TBSP FRESH CILANTRO, CHOPPED TO GARNISH

1/2 CUP CHOPPED TOMATOES

1/2 CUP WATER

1/4 CUP GREEK YOGURT (OPTIONAL)

1. In a skillet, add the oil and heat on a medium heat.
2. Add the onion and garlic and stir for 5 minutes until soft.
3. Add the cumin, turmeric and garam masala and stir to release the aromas.
4. Now add the chili to the pan along with the chickpeas and cauliflower. Stir to coat in the spices.
5. Pour in the tomatoes and water and reduce the heat to simmer for 30 minutes or until chickpeas soft.
6. Garnish with cilantro to serve as well as a dollop of yogurt if desired.

Per Serving: 410 Calories, 19G Protein, 59G Carbohydrates, 11g Fat

GARLIC STUFFED MUSHROOMS

SERVES 2 /   PREP TIME: 5 MINUTES /   COOK TIME: 15 MINUTES

Portabella mushrooms are a meal in themselves.

---

4 LARGE PORTABELLA MUSHROOMS

1/2 CUP OF QUINOA, COOKED

2 GARLIC CLOVES, MINCED

1 BEEF TOMATO, SLICED

1 TBSP OF EXTRA VIRGIN OLIVE OIL

1 TBSP THYME

PINCH OF BLACK PEPPER

---

1. Preheat the broiler to a medium high heat.
2. Remove the stems from the mushrooms and place to one side.
3. Combine the cooked quinoa, garlic, tomato, oil, black pepper, mushroom stems and thyme and add to a food processor to blitz.
4. Place the portabella mushrooms on a baking sheet and lightly brush with olive oil.
5. Stack the mushroom caps with the quinoa mixture.
6. Place under the broiler for 10 minutes, then serve hot.

Per Serving: 406 Calories, 15G Protein, 63G Carbohydrates, 11g Fat

CREAMY WALNUT PENNE

SERVES 2 / PREP TIME: 5 MINUTES / COOK TIME: 20 MINUTES

A low fat creamy sauce goes brilliantly with the nutty textures.

---

1 CUP 100% WHOLEGRAIN PASTA

1 CUP ALMOND MILK

1/2 CUP COTTAGE CHEESE

1/4 CUP OF WALNUTS, COARSELY CHOPPED

1 TBSP TARRAGON

PINCH OF BLACK PEPPER

1/2 CUP SPINACH LEAVES

---

1. Boil a large saucepan of water on a high heat.
2. Add the pasta and cook following directions on the package.
3. While the pasta is cooking, prepare the sauce:
4. Whisk the cottage cheese with the almond milk until the lumps have gone (alternatively use a food processor).
5. Once the pasta is cooked, drain and add the white sauce over a low heat.
6. Toss through until the pasta is well coated and the sauce is hot.
7. Add the walnuts, spinach and tarragon and stir well until the spinach has wilted.
8. Transfer onto a serving plate and sprinkle with a little black pepper.

Per Serving: 292 Calories, 16G Protein, 28G Carbohydrates, 13g Fat

PUMPKIN & PINE NUT CASSEROLE

SERVES 4 / PREP TIME: 10 MINUTES / COOK TIME: 50 MINUTES

Hearty stew with a crunchy topping.

2 TBSP EXTRA VIRGIN OLIVE OIL	3 TBSP PINE NUTS
1 CUP RED ONION, CHOPPED	1 TBSP PAPRIKA
1 PUMPKIN	1 TBSP THYME
1 TSP BLACK PEPPER	1 TSP BLACK PEPPER
1 TSP CHILI POWDER	1 CUP VEG STOCK
1 BAY LEAF	1/2 CUP CHOPPED TOMATOES
	2 CUP COOKED QUINOA

1. Prepare the pumpkin by using a sharp knife to remove the 'lid' and then scooping out the flesh with a spoon/fork.
2. Heat the oil in a pot over a medium to high heat and add the red onion for 5 minutes.
3. Season with herbs and spices before adding in pumpkin flesh and stirring for 5 minutes.
4. Add tomatoes, bay leaf and stock, cover and simmer for 40-45 minutes or until pumpkin soft.
5. Meanwhile preheat the oven to its highest temperature.
6. Serve with your choice of brown rice or quinoa and scatter the pine nuts over the top.

Per Serving: 438 Calories, 13G Protein, 64G Carbohydrates, 14g Fat

CHINESE TEMPAH STIR FRY

SERVES 2 / PREP TIME: 5 MINUTES / COOK TIME: 15 MINUTES

Tempah is a great source of protein

---

1 TBSP COCONUT OIL

1 CLOVE GARLIC, MINCED

1 THUMB SIZED PIECE FRESH GINGER, MINCED

1 PACK TEMPAH, SLICED

1/2 CUP GREEN ONIONS

1/2 CUP BEAN SPROUTS

1/2 CUP BABY CORN/SWEETCORN

1 CUP BROWN RICE, COOKED

---

1. Heat the oil in a skillet or wok on a high heat and add the garlic, spices and ginger.
2. Cook for 1 minute.
3. Now add the tempah and cook for 5-6 minutes before adding the bean sprouts and baby corn for a further 10 minutes.
4. Now add the green onions and serve over brown rice.

Per Serving: 392 Calories, 19G Protein, 42G Carbohydrates, 20g Fat

AESTHETIC ASPARAGUS & BEETROOT TART

SERVES 4 / PREP TIME: 5 MINUTES / COOK TIME: 25 MINUTES

Pastry-free tart with the crisp freshness of the asparagus with the sweet edge of the beetroot.

---

1 TBSP COCONUT OIL	1 CUP COCONUT MILK
1/2 CUP ASPARAGUS	1 TSP BLACK PEPPER
1/2 CUP COOKED BEETROOT	
6 EGGS	

---

1. Preheat the broiler to a medium heat.
2. Whisk the eggs and coconut milk in a separate bowl.
3. On a medium heat, heat the coconut oil in an oven proof (steel) frying pan, adding in the asparagus and beetroot and sautéing for 5 minutes.
4. Add the egg mix to the pan with the vegetables in and continue to cook on the stove (low heat) for 7 minutes until it becomes light and bubbly.
5. Finish the tart in its pan under the broiler for a further 5 -10 minutes or until crispy on the top and cooked through.
6. Slice and serve hot or allow to cool and serve chilled from the fridge!

Per Serving: 156 Calories, 10G Protein, 3G Carbohydrates, 11g Fat

RAISIN & ROOT VEG STEW

SERVES 2 / PREP TIME: 5 MINUTES / COOK TIME: 35 MINUTES

A vegetarian take on this classic dish.

2 TBSP OLIVE OIL	1/2 CUP CARROTS, PEELED AND DICED
1 ONION, DICED	2 PARSNIPS, PEELED AND DICED
2 TURNIPS, PEELED AND DICED	1 SWEET POTATO, PEELED AND DICED
2 CLOVES OF GARLIC	2 CUPS HOMEMADE VEGETABLE STOCK
1 TSP GROUND CUMIN	1/4 CUP FRESH PARSLEY, CHOPPED
1/2 TSP GROUND GINGER	1/4 CUP RAISINS
1/2 TSP GROUND CINNAMON	1 CUP COOKED QUINOA
1/4 TSP CAYENNE PEPPER	

1. In a large pot, heat the oil on a medium high heat before sautéing the onion for 4-5 minutes until soft.
2. Add the turnip, sweet potato and parsnip and cook for 10 minutes or until golden brown.
3. Add the garlic, cumin, ginger, cinnamon, and cayenne pepper, cooking for a further 3 minutes.
4. Add the carrots, raisins and stock to the pot and then bring to the boil.
5. Turn the heat down to a medium heat, cover and simmer for 20 minutes.
6. Garnish with the parsley and serve with the quinoa.

Per Serving: 642 Calories, 15G Protein, 105G Carbohydrates, 15g Fat

SPANISH PAELLA

SERVES 2 / PREP TIME: 10 MINUTES / COOK TIME: 25 MINUTES

A delicious protein packed meal

1 TBSP EXTRA VIRGIN OLIVE OIL	1 LEMON
1/2 RED BELL PEPPER, CHOPPED	1 TSP PAPRIKA
1/2 YELLOW BELL PEPPER, CHOPPED	1 TSP OREGANO (DRIED)
1/2 ZUCCHINI, CHOPPED	1 TSP PARSLEY (DRIED)
1/2 RED ONION, CHOPPED	1 CUP HOMEMADE VEGETABLE STOCK
1 CUP BROWN RICE	1 CUP RED LENTILS, SOAKED

1. Add rice and lentils to a pot of cold water and cook for 15 minutes.
2. Drain the water, cover the pan and leave to one side.
3. Heat the oil in a skillet and add the bell pepper,s onion and zucchini, sautéing for 5 minutes.
4. To the pan, add the rice, lentils, herb, spices and juice of the lemon along with the vegetable stock/water.
5. Cover and turn heat right down and allow to simmer for 15-20 minutes.
6. Serve hot.

Per Serving: 345 Calories, 12G Protein, 50G Carbohydrates, 9g Fat

KINO KEDGEREE

SERVES 2 / PREP TIME: 5 MINUTES / COOK TIME: 30 MINUTES

A vegetarian take on this classic dish.

---

2 ONIONS, CUT INTO QUARTERS

1/2 CUP BROCCOLI

1/4 CAULIFLOWER

1 TBSP EXTRA VIRGIN OLIVE OIL

1 TBSP CURRY POWDER

1 CUP BROWN RICE, RINSED THOROUGHLY

2 EGGS

1 TSP BLACK PEPPER

1 TBSP FRESH CHIVES, CHOPPED

---

1. Preheat the oven to 375°f/190°c/Gas Mark 5.
2. Add the vegetables to an oven dish and toss together.
3. Drizzle with oil and sprinkle with curry powder and pepper - toss to coat.
4. Bake in the oven for 30 minutes, stirring occasionally.
5. Meanwhile add the rice to a pot of cold water and bring to the boil over a high heat.
6. Simmer for 15 minutes until rice has nearly soaked up all of the water.
7. Turn the heat to the lowest temperature and cover the pan for a further 5 minutes until light and fluffy.
8. Boil a separate pan of water and add the eggs for 7 minutes.
9. Run under the cold tap, crack and peel the eggs before cutting in half.
10. Toss the rice with the roasted vegetables and top with eggs and chopped chives.
11. Serve hot!

Per Serving: 287 Calories, 10G Protein, 33G Carbohydrates, 12g Fat

ZESTY ZUCCHINI PASTA & PROTEIN PEAS

SERVES 2 / PREP TIME: 10 MINUTES / COOK TIME: 40 MINUTES

Gloriously healthy homemade pasta with a crunchy topping.

---

1 CUP FROZEN PEAS

1 TBSP FRESH MINT, CHOPPED

1/2 CUP GREEK YOGURT

4 ZUCCHINIS, PEELED AND SLICED VERTICALLY TO MAKE NOODLES (USE A SPIRALIZER)

1 TSP BLACK PEPPER

1 TSP HONEY

1 TSP RED CHILI FLAKES

1 TBSP EXTRA VIRGIN OLIVE OIL

1/2 CUP ARUGULA

1/2 LEMON, JUICED

---

1. Add the peas, mint, pepper, chili, honey and yogurt to a food processor and blend until smooth.
2. Meanwhile, heat a pan of water on a high heat and bring to the boil.
3. Add the zucchini noodles and turn the heat down to simmer for 3-4 minutes.
4. Remove from the heat and place in a bowl of cold water immediately.
5. Serve zucchini noodles with the pea dressing.
6. Mix the arugula with the lemon juice and serve on the side.
7. Enjoy!

Per Serving: 219 Calories, 9G Protein, 18G Carbohydrates, 12g Fat

SCALLION & GOATS CHEESE PANCAKES

SERVES 2 / PREP TIME: 5 MINUTES / COOK TIME: 10 MINUTES

Enjoy pancakes the savoury way.

2 EGGS	1/2 CUP ROLLED OATS
1/2 CUP RICE MILK (UNENRICHED)	1 TBSP COCONUT OIL
1/2 CUP WATER	1/4 CUP SCALLIONS, FINELY DICED
1 TSP BLACK PEPPER	1/4 CUP GOATS' CHEESE, CRUMBLED
1 SCOOP UNFLAVORED PROTEIN POWDER	1 TSP THYME

1. In a medium bowl add the eggs, milk, water, and pepper together until combined.
2. Add the oats and protein powder to the mix and whisk into a smooth paste.
3. Use a food processor for convenience here.
4. Take 2 tbsp of the oil and melt in a skillet over a medium heat.
5. Add 1/2 pancake mixture to form a round pancake shape.
6. Cook for 4-5 minutes until the bottom is light brown and easily comes away from the pan with the spatula.
7. Flip and add half the scallions and crumbled cheese over the top before cooking for a further 4 minutes.
8. Fold and serve warm - the cheese should have melted and the onions will be warm but still crunchy.
9. Serve and repeat with the rest of the ingredients.

Per Serving: 334 Calories, 19G Protein, 23G Carbohydrates, 16g Fat

CHILI & HONEY SQUASH WITH CRISPY KALE & TOFU

SERVES 2 / PREP TIME: 10 MINUTES / COOK TIME: 50 MINUTES

Protein and vitamin rich.

---

1 BUTTERNUT SQUASH

1 TBSP RAW HONEY

1 TBSP CHILI FLAKES

2 CUPS KALE

4 GARLIC CLOVES, WHOLE

1 CUP FIRM TOFU, PRESSED

---

1. Preheat the oven to 375°f/190°c/Gas Mark 5.
2. Peel and slice the butternut squash as thin as possible.
3. Layer on a lined baking dish and drizzle with honey.
4. Sprinkle chili flakes over the top and use a spatula or spoon to toss and coat thoroughly.
5. Add to the oven for 35-40 minutes.
6. Meanwhile, on a separate baking tray, layer the kale and tofu with the garlic cloves scattered on top.
7. Sprinkle with nutmeg and add to the oven for 30 minutes or until crispy.

Per Serving: 189 Calories, 9G Protein, 33G Carbohydrates, 3G Fat

LIME & GINGER TEMPAH

SERVES 2 / PREP TIME: 10 MINUTES / COOK TIME: 40 MINUTES

Chunky tempah with a kick.

---

1 PACK TEMPAH

1 LIME, JUICED

1 TBSP GINGER, GRATED

1 TSP SOY SAUCE

1 TSP COCONUT OIL

1 CUP SUGAR SNAP PEAS/EDAMAME

1 TSP CHILI FLAKES

---

1. Mix the oil, soy sauce, lime juice and ginger and marinate the tempah for as long as possible.
2. Preheat the broiler to a medium heat.
3. Add tempah to a lined baking tray and broil for 10-15 minutes or until hot through.
4. Meanwhile, boil a pot of water over a high heat.
5. Once boiling, add the sugar snap peas/edamame to a steamer/colander over the top of the pan.
6. Lower the heat and steam for 10 minutes.
7. Remove and sprinkle with chili flakes.
8. Serve the tempah with the crunchy peas and enjoy.

Per Serving: 247 Calories, 13G Protein, 25G Carbohydrates, 15G Fat

SEAFOOD

CALAMARI & SHRIMP PAELLA

SERVES 2 / PREP TIME: 5 MINUTES / COOK TIME: 10 MINUTES

Mouthwatering!

6 OZ FROZEN COOKED SHRIMP	1 TSP PAPRIKA
1 CUP CALAMARI, FRESH OR FROZEN	1 TSP CHILI FLAKES
1 TBSP OLIVE OIL	1 TBSP OREGANO
1 RED ONION, CHOPPED	1 CUP COOKED BROWN RICE
1 GARLIC CLOVE, CHOPPED	1/2 CUP FROZEN PEAS

1. Heat olive oil in a pan on a medium to high heat.
2. Add the onion and garlic and then fry for 2-3 minutes until soft.
3. Add the calamari and sauté for 5-10 minutes or until hot through.
4. Now add the shrimp and sauté for a further 5 minutes or until hot through.
5. Now add the herbs and spices, rice and frozen peas with 1/2 cup boiling water.
6. Stir until everything is warm and the water has been absorbed.
7. Plate up and serve.

Per Serving: 313 Calories, 27G Protein, 33G Carbohydrates, 11G Fat

SALMON FILLET & PESTO MASH

SERVES 2 / PREP TIME: 5 MINUTES / COOK TIME: 30 MINUTES

Add a little twist to your normal salmon dish.

2X SALMON FILLETS

1 TSP BLACK PEPPER

1 TBSP EXTRA VIRGIN OLIVE OIL

FOR THE MASH:

2 SWEET POTATOES, PEELED AND CUBED

FOR THE PESTO:

1/2 CUP FRESH BASIL

1/2 CUP FRESH SPINACH

1 TSP BLACK PEPPER

1/4 CUP EXTRA VIRGIN OLIVE OIL

1 GARLIC CLOVE, MINCED

---

1. Prepare the pesto by blending all the ingredients for the pesto in a food processor or grinding with a pestle and mortar. Place to one side.
2. Boil a pan of water on a high heat and add the sweet potatoes.
3. Allow to boil for 20-25 minutes or until very soft.
4. Drain and use a potato masher to mash the sweet potatoes.
5. Fold the pesto through the mash.
6. Now grab a skillet and heat the oil over a medium to high heat.
7. Sprinkle black pepper over the salmon fillets and score the skin of the fish a few times with a sharp knife.
8. Add the fish to the very hot pan with the skin side down.
9. Cook for 7-8 minutes and turn over (this will allow the skin to turn crispy and golden).
10. Cook for a further 3-4 minutes or until cooked through.
11. Remove fillets from the skillet and allow to rest.
12. Serve with the pesto mash and a side of greens.

Per Serving: 506 Calories, 28G Protein, 22G Carbohydrates, 35G Fat

FENNEL & OLIVE SEA BASS

SERVES 2 / PREP TIME: 5 MINUTES / COOK TIME: 15 MINUTES

Fuel up with this tasty fish dish!

2X SEA BASS FILLETS	1 GARLIC CLOVE
1 TSP BLACK PEPPER	1/4 CUP OLIVES
1 TSP EXTRA VIRGIN OLIVE OIL	2 GREEN ONION STEMS, SLICED
1 FENNEL BULB, SLICED	1 LEMON
	1 CUP COUSCOUS

1. Preheat the oven to 375°f/190°c/Gas Mark 5.
2. Sprinkle black pepper over the Sea Bass and score the skin of the fish a few times with a sharp knife.
3. Slice the fennel bulb and garlic clove.
4. Tear off two squares of baking paper or tin foil and add half of the fennel bulb, garlic, olives and green onions stems to the centre of the paper.
5. Place the sea bass fillet on top squeeze half the lemon juice in each parcel.
6. Add the rest of the lemon to each parcel.
7. Fold up loosely and add to the oven for 12-15 minutes or until fish is thoroughly cooked through and flakes easily.
8. Meanwhile, add boiling water to your couscous, cover and allow to steam.
9. Once it has soaked up the water, use your fork to fluff the couscous.
10. Add a little salt and pepper and olive oil and then serve the seabass, vegetables and all the lovely juices from the parcel over the couscous.

Per Serving: 278 Calories, 25G Protein, 23G Carbohydrates, 9G Fat

BULK-UP SARDINES WITH LEMON, GARLIC & PARSLEY

SERVES 2 / PREP TIME: 5 MINUTES / COOK TIME: 15 MINUTES

European inspired sardines.

---

8 OZ SARDINES, FRESH OR CANNED

1 TSP BLACK PEPPER

1 TBSP EXTRA VIRGIN OLIVE OIL

1 LEMON, JUICED

1/4 CUP WILD GARLIC (OR 2 GARLIC CLOVES)

1/4 CUP FRESH PARSLEY, CHOPPED

---

1. Mix the olive oil, pepper, parsley and garlic in a bowl.
2. Marinate the sardines in the mixture for as long as possible.
3. When ready to cook, preheat the broiler to a medium heat.
4. Add the sardines to a lined baking dish and place under the broiler for 8-12 minutes or until thoroughly cooked through.
5. Enjoy!

Per Serving: 215 Calories, 20G Protein, 1G Carbohydrates, 14G Fat

COD, PEA & SPINACH RISOTTO

SERVES 2 / PREP TIME: 4 MINUTES / COOK TIME: 40 MINUTES

A healthy yet delicious risotto dish.

2X SMOKED COD FILLETS SKINLESS, BONELESS	1 CUP FRESH SPINACH LEAVES
1 TBSP EXTRA VIRGIN OLIVE OIL	1 CUP OF FROZEN PEAS
1 WHITE ONION, FINELY DICED	3 TBSP LOW FAT GREEK YOGURT (OPTIONAL)
2 CUPS BROWN RICE	A PINCH OF BLACK PEPPER
4 CUPS VEGETABLE STOCK	4 LEMON WEDGES
	1 CUP OF ARUGULA

1. Heat the oil in a large pan on a medium heat.
2. Sauté the chopped onion for 5 minutes until soft before adding in the rice and
3. stirring for 1-2 minutes.
4. Add half of the stock and stir slowly.
5. Slowly add the rest of the stock whilst continuously stirring for up to 20-30 minutes (this is a bit of a workout!)
6. Stir in the spinach and peas to the risotto.
7. Place the fish on top of the rice, cover and steam for 10 minutes.
8. Use your fork to break up the fish fillets and stir into the rice with the yogurt.
9. Sprinkle with freshly ground pepper to serve and a squeeze of fresh lemon.
10. Garnish with the lemon wedges and serve with the arugula.

Per Serving: 527 Calories, 34G Protein, 74G Carbohydrates, 12G Fat

RAINBOW TROUT

SERVES 1 / PREP TIME: 5 MINUTES / COOK TIME: 15 MINUTES

Multiply your reps with this dish!

1 WHOLE TROUT, GUTTED BY YOUR FISH-MONGER

1/4 RED PEPPER, DICED

1/4 YELLOW PEPPER, DICED

1/4 GREEN PEPPER, DICED

1 LIME, JUICED

1/4 CUP COOKED COUSCOUS

1 TSP THYME

1 TSP OREGANO

1 TSP BLACK PEPPER

1 TBSP EXTRA VIRGIN OLIVE OIL

1. Preheat the broiler on a high heat.
2. Lightly oil a baking tray.
3. Mix all of the ingredients apart from the trout and lime.
4. Slice the trout lengthways (there should be an opening here from where it was gutted) and stuff the mixed ingredients inside.
5. Squeeze the lime juice over the fish and then place the lime wedges on the tray.
6. Place under the broiler on the baking tray and broil for 15-20 minutes or until fish is thoroughly cooked through and flakes easily.
7. Enjoy with a salad of your choice.

Per Serving: 330 Calories, 20G Protein, 20G Carbohydrates, 19G Fat

LANGOUSTINE & SWEET POTATO FRIES

SERVES 2 / **PREP TIME: 10 MINUTES** / **COOK TIME: 20 MINUTES**

Posh body building grub!

FOR THE FRIES:

2 LARGE SWEET POTATOES, CUT INTO FRIES

1 TSP OF CUMIN

1 TBSP OF EXTRA VIRGIN OLIVE OIL

1/2 TSP OF BLACK PEPPER

1/2 TSP OF PAPRIKA

1 DASH OF CAYENNE PEPPER

FOR THE LANGOUSTINE:

2 CUPS OF WHOLE LANGOUSTINES

1 TBSP GHEE

1 TBSP FRESH PARSLEY

1 LEMON

---

1. Preheat oven to 375°F/190 °C/Gas Mark 5.
2. Add the sweet potato strips into a large bowl.
3. Drizzle with some olive oil.
4. Sprinkle the rest of the ingredients over the top.
5. Toss together gently to evenly coat the potatoes.
6. Get a baking sheet and arrange the coated potatoes into a thin layer.
7. Bake for around 30 minutes or until cooked through.
8. Meanwhile, prepare your langoustines by boiling a pan of water non a high heat and boiling langoustines for 5 minutes.
9. Remove from heat and chop the langoustines in half (lengthways). Remove the vein from the middle with a sharp knife.
10. Mix the ghee, parsley and lemon.
11. Heat a skillet on a medium to high heat and add the langoustine before drizzling the parsley and ghee over the top and leave to cook for 10 minutes or until cooked through. Serve with the sweet potato fries!

Per Serving: 357 Calories, 13G Protein, 22G Carbohydrates, 14G Fat

TOMATO & WALNUT SOLE

SERVES 2 / PREP TIME: 5 MINUTES / COOK TIME: 15 MINUTES

The crunchy topping on this fish makes it stand out from the crowd and the kale is rich in vitamins and iron.

---

2 TSP EXTRA VIRGIN OLIVE OIL

1/2 CUP WALNUTS

1 EGG WHITE

2X SOLE FILLETS, SKINLESS

2 TSP WHOLE GRAIN MUSTARD

1 HEAD OF KALE, CHOPPED

1 CLOVE OF GARLIC, MASHED

1 CUP CANNED CHOPPED TOMATOES,

---

1. Preheat oven to 350°f/170°c/Gas Mark 4.
2. Lightly oil a baking sheet with 1 tsp extra virgin olive oil.
3. Mix the walnuts and egg white together.
4. Spread a thin layer of the mustard over the fish and then dip into the walnut mixture.
5. Transfer to baking dish.
6. Bake for 12 minutes or until cooked through.
7. Meanwhile, heat 1 tsp oil in a skillet on a medium heat and sauté the garlic for 30 seconds, adding in the tomatoes and kale for a further 5 minutes.
8. Serve the fish with the tomato sauce over the top.

Per Serving: 492 Calories, 30G Protein, 16G Carbohydrates, 36G Fat

SALMON BURGERS WITH AVOCADO

SERVES 2 / PREP TIME: 5 MINUTES / COOK TIME: 10 MINUTES

Salmon burgers are delicious and packed with healthy oils and fats.

---

1 BEATEN FREE RANGE EGG

2 CANS OF WILD SALMON, DRAINED

2 SCALLIONS, CHOPPED

2 TBSP COCONUT OIL

1 TSP DILL, CHOPPED

1 AVOCADO

1 LIME

1 CUP COOKED BROWN RICE

1 CUP SPINACH, WASHED

---

1. Combine the salmon, egg, dill, scallions and 1 tbsp oil in a bowl, mixing well with your hands to form 2 patties.
2. Heat 1 tbsp oil over a medium heat in a skillet and cook the patties for 4 minutes each side until firm and browned.
3. Squeeze the lime juice over the top and flip once more.
4. Peel and slice the avocado.
5. Stack the burgers with the avocado sliced on top and a helping of spinach leaves and serve brown rice.

Per Serving: 611 Calories, 62G Protein, 34G Carbohydrates, 34G Fat

HEAVY HADDOCK & BEAN STEW

SERVES 2 / PREP TIME: 10 MINUTES / COOK TIME: 30 MINUTES

A great warm up!

2X HADDOCK FILLETS

A PINCH OF BLACK PEPPER

1 CUP HOMEMADE CHICKEN BROTH

1 CUP CANNED TOMATOES

1 TSP OLIVE OIL

1 CARROT, DICED

2 TSP CILANTRO, FINELY CHOPPED

1/4 CUP TURKEY BACON

1/2 CUP CHICKPEAS

1 TSP PARSLEY

1 TSP CILANTRO

---

1. Rub the fish with pepper.
2. In a large saucepan, heat the oil on a medium heat and cook the carrot and turkey bacon for 5 minutes.
3. Add the chopped tomatoes, stock, cod fillet, chickpeas and herbs.
4. Add the rest of the reserved chicken stock and simmer for 20-30 minutes.
5. Serve hot!

Per Serving: 334 Calories, 28G Protein, 19G Carbohydrates, 14G Fat

ASIAN SPICED HALIBUT

SERVES 2   PREP TIME: 5 MINUTES   COOK TIME: 20 MINUTES

Kick start your workout.

2X HALIBUT FILLETS	1 RED CHILLI, DICED
A PINCH OF BLACK PEPPER	2 GREEN ONIONS, SLICED
2 GARLIC CLOVES, PRESSED	1 BOK CHOY PLANT
2 TBSP COCONUT OIL	1 LIME LEAF
1 LEMON, JUICED	1 TBSP FRESH BASIL

1. Preheat oven to 400°f/190°c/Gas Mark 5.
2. Add half of the ingredients into baking paper and fold into a parcel.
3. Add to the oven for 15-20 minutes or until fish thoroughly cooked through.
4. Serve this with your favorite vegetables, salad or even sweet potatoes.

Per Serving: 354 Calories, 42G Protein, 2G Carbohydrates, 18G Fat

TERRIFIC TUNA NICOISE

SERVES 2 / PREP TIME: 5 MINUTES / COOK TIME: 25 MINUTES

King of the salads!

2X TUNA STEAKS, EACH 1 INCH THICK	1/2 CUP WATER
2 TBSP OLIVE OIL,	1 LEMON, JUICED
2 EGGS	1 TSP FRESH PARSLEY, CHOPPED
1 TSP BLACK PEPPER	1/2 ICEBERG LETTUCE (OR SIMILAR)
1 GARLIC CLOVE, CRUSHED	1 TSP BALSAMIC VINEGAR
1 TBSP CAPERS	10 CHERRY TOMATOES
1/2 CUP GREEN BEANS	1/4 RED ONION, THINLY SLICED

1. Prepare the salad by washing and slicing the lettuce, tomatoes and onion and tossing together.
2. Mix 1 tbsp oil with the lemon juice, parsley and capers to form your salad dressing. Place to one side.
3. Boil a pan of water on a high heat then lower to simmer and add eggs for 6 minutes. Steam the green beans over the pan in a steamer/colander for the 6 minutes.
4. Meanwhile, brush the fish with 1 tbsp oil and then season with pepper.
5. Heat a skillet on a medium heat and sauté the garlic for 2-3 minutes.
6. Add the tuna steaks for about 2-3 minutes each side for medium-rare. (Add 1 minute each side for medium and 2 minutes each side for medium well).
7. Remove tuna from the skillet and allow to rest whilst you dress the salad with the dressing prepared earlier and toss through.
8. Rinse the eggs under cold water and peel before slicing in half.
9. Slice the tuna steaks and add to the salad with the eggs and green beans.

Per Serving: 325 Calories, 42G Protein, 7G Carbohydrates, 18G Fat

SESAME MONKFISH & FRUIT SALSA

SERVES 2 / PREP TIME: 5 MINUTES / COOK TIME: 20 MINUTES

This fun tropical dish combines a great-tasting fish with a tangy salsa.

FOR THE SALSA:

1 CUP FRESH MANGO, PEELED AND CUBED

1/2 RED CHILI, FINELY CHOPPED

1 LIME, JUICED

2 TSP CILANTRO, CHOPPED

1 ONION, FINELY CHOPPED

FOR THE FISH:

2 MONKFISH FILLETS

2 TSP OLIVE OIL

2 TBSP SESAME SEEDS

1. Get a bowl and mix all of the ingredients for the salsa.
2. Drizzle 1 tbsp olive oil on the fillets and coat each side with the sesame seeds.
3. Heat 1 tbsp oil over a medium heat and then sauté the fillets for about 8 minutes each side or until the flesh flakes away.
4. Serve with the salsa on the side.

Per Serving: 317 Calories, 18G Protein, 16G Carbohydrates, 18G Fat

GINGER & HONEY MAHI-MAHI WITH ORANGE SALAD

SERVES 2 / PREP TIME: 5 MINUTES / COOK TIME: 20 MINUTES

This fun tropical dish combines a great-tasting fish with a tangy salsa.

FOR THE SALAD:	FOR THE FISH:
1 ORANGE, SEGMENTED	2X MAHI MAHI FILLETS
1/4 RED CHILI, FINELY CHOPPED	2 TSP PEANUT OIL
1 CUP SPINACH LEAVES	1 TSP GINGER, GRATED
1 TSP BALSAMIC VINEGAR	1 TBSP HONEY
1 TBSP OLIVE OIL	1 TBSP BALSAMIC VINEGAR

1. Get a bowl and mix all of the ingredients for the salad.
2. Mix the ginger, honey, oil and balsamic vinegar and then brush over the mahi-mahi.
3. Heat a skillet over a medium heat and then sauté the fillets for about 8 minutes each side or until the flesh flakes away.
4. Serve with the salad on the side. Season with salt and pepper to taste.

Per Serving: 427 Calories, 30G Protein, 26G Carbohydrates, 20G Fat

SMOKED TROUT FISH CAKES

SERVES 2 / PREP TIME: 5 MINUTES / COOK TIME: 35 MINUTES

Great for lunch or dinner.

---

2 LARGE SWEET POTATOES, PEELED AND CUBED

3 TBSP EXTRA VIRGIN OLIVE OIL

1 LEEK, CHOPPED

4 TSP DILL, CHOPPED

1 TBSP GRATED ORANGE PEEL

1 PACK SMOKED TROUT, SLICED

1`/3 CUP LOW FAT GREEK YOGURT (OPTIONAL)

---

1. Preheat oven to 325°f/150°c/Gas Mark 3.
2. Lightly grease 2 ramekins or circular baking dishes with a little olive oil.
3. Heat the rest of the oil in a skillet over medium heat, and sauté the leeks and the potatoes for 5 minutes.
4. Lower the heat and cook for another 10 minutes until tender.
5. Transfer the potatoes and leeks to a separate bowl and crush with a fork to form a mash (alternatively use a potato masher).
6. Add the dill, orange peel and the trout and mix well.
7. Fill the ramekins with half the mixture each, patting to compact.
8. Bake for 15 minutes and remove.

Tip the ramekin out onto a plate, season and top with a dollop of Greek yogurt (optional).

Per Serving: 529 Calories, 23G Protein, 47G Carbohydrates, 26G Fat

SCALLOPS WITH CAULIFLOWER & CHILI

SERVES 2 / PREP TIME: 5 MINUTES / COOK TIME: 10 MINUTES

We all deserve a treat now and then!

6 QUEEN OR KING SCALLOPS (ROW ON)   1 LIME, JUICED

1 TBSP COCONUT OIL

1/4 CAULIFLOWER

1 RED CHILLI, DICED

A PINCH OF BLACK PEPPER

1. Wash the cauliflower and remove any leaves. Use a sharp knife to cut very thin slices of cauliflower.
2. Add oil to a pan over a medium heat and add the cauliflower slices and chili for 3-4 minutes. Remove and place to one side.
3. Add the scallops to the same pan and squeeze over the lime juice.
4. Sauté for about 1 minute each side until lightly golden.
5. Plate up the cauliflower slices and place the scallops on top before seasoning with black pepper to taste.

Per Serving: 164 Calories, 18G Protein, 6G Carbohydrates, 8G Fat

COCONUT SHRIMP & NOODLES

SERVES 2 / PREP TIME: 10 MINUTES / COOK TIME:15 MINUTES

Crunchy shrimp with sweet & sour sauce.

8OZ SHRIMP, PEELED AND DE VEINED	A PINCH OF BLACK PEPPER TO TASTE
1/4 CUP COCONUT FLOUR	1 CUP COOKED NOODLES
1/2 TSP CAYENNE PEPPER	1 TSP SOY SAUCE
1 TSP GARLIC POWDER	1 TSP STEVIA
2 BEATEN FREE RANGE EGGS	1/4 CUP PINEAPPLE
1/2 CUP SHREDDED COCONUT	1 TSP VINEGAR
1/4 CUP ALMOND FLOUR	1 TBSP KETCHUP

1. Preheat oven to 400°f/200°c/Gas Mark 6.
2. Line a baking sheet with parchment paper.
3. Mix the coconut flour, cayenne pepper, and garlic powder in a bowl.
4. In a separate bowl, whisk the eggs.
5. In a third bowl, add the shredded coconut, almond flour and pepper.
6. Dip the shrimp into each dish in consecutive order, and then place on the baking sheet and bake for 10-15 minutes or until cooked through. Remove and place to one side.
7. Heat the soy sauce, ketchup, stevia, vinegar and pineapple with 1/2 cup water in a pan over a medium heat, stirring occasionally or until reduced.
8. Add to the cooked noodles in a pan until heated through and serve with the coconut shrimp on top.
9. Try with a side of broccoli.

Per Serving: 455 Calories, 44G Protein, 52G Carbohydrates, 15G Fat

SPICY SWORDFISH STEAKS

SERVES 2 / PREP TIME: 35 MINUTES / COOK TIME: 40 MINUTES

If you can't get hold of swordfish, try this with tuna, shark or monkfish.

2X SWORDFISH STEAKS, SKINLESS

2 TBSP ONION POWDER

2 TSP CHILI POWDER

1 GARLIC CLOVE, MINCED

1/4 CUP WORCESTERSHIRE SAUCE

1 TBSP GROUND BLACK PEPPER

2 TBSP THYME, CHOPPED

---

1. In a bowl, mix all of the seasoning's and spices to form a paste before setting aside.
2. Spread a thin layer of paste on both sides of the fish, cover and chill for 30 minutes (If possible).
3. Preheat oven to 325°f/150°c/Gas Mark 3.
4. Bake the fish in parchment paper for 30-40 minutes, until well cooked.
5. Serve on a bed of quinoa or wholegrain couscous and your favorite salad.

Per Serving: 455 Calories, 44G Protein, 52G Carbohydrates, 15G Fat

THAI TRAINING BROTH

SERVES 2 / PREP TIME: 5 MINUTES / COOK TIME: 25 MINUTES

Aromatic and spicy!

2X COD/HADDOCK FILLETS	1 TBSP OLIVE OIL
1 TSP BLACK PEPPER	1 CUP PAK CHOI
1 CUP HOMEMADE CHICKEN/VEG BROTH	1/4 CUP SWEETCORN
1 CUP WATER	1 TBSP GINGER, MINCED
1 TSP COCONUT OIL	1 CUP NOODLES
1 TSP FIVE-SPICE POWDER	1 GREEN ONION, THINLY SLICED
	2 TSP CILANTRO, FINELY CHOPPED

1. In a bowl, combine pepper, 1/2 cup chicken broth, 1 cup water, coconut oil and spice blend.
2. Mix together and place to one side.
3. In a large saucepan, heat the oil on a medium heat and cook the pak choy and ginger for about 2 minutes until the bok choy is green.
4. Add the rest of the reserved chicken stock and heat through.
5. Add the noodles and stir, bringing to a simmer.
6. Add the green onion, sweetcorn and the fish and cook for 10-15 minutes until fish is tender.
7. Add the fish, noodles and vegetables into serving bowls and pour the broth over the top.
8. Garnish with the cilantro.

Per Serving: 408 Calories, 35G Protein, 25G Carbohydrates, 15G Fat

GARLIC & LEMON SHRIMP LINGUINE

SERVES 2 / PREP TIME: 35 MINUTES / COOK TIME: 20 MINUTES

Amazing!

---

12 OZ SHRIMP, FRESH OR FROZEN

1 GARLIC CLOVE, MINCED

10 CHERRY TOMATOES, SLICED IN HALF

1 TSP OREGANO

1 CUP WHOLE WHEAT LINGUINE

2 TBSP OLIVE OIL

1/4 CUP GREEN ONIONS, CHOPPED

1/2 LEMON, JUICED

---

1. If shrimp is frozen, allow to thoroughly defrost before cooking.
2. Heat a pan of water over a medium to high heat.
3. Once boiling, add linguine and lower heat to a simmer.
4. Cook according to package directions.
5. Meanwhile, heat 1 tbsp oil in a skillet over a medium heat.
6. Add the garlic, onions and tomatoes and sauté for 1-2 minutes.
7. Now add the prawns and cook thoroughly according to package directions.
8. Squeeze 1/4 lemon juice into the pan and shake gently for 1-2 minutes.
9. Drain the pasta and pour the shrimp, vegetables and all the lovely juices over the linguine and toss.
10. Drizzle the rest of the olive oil and lemon juice over the linguine to serve.

Per Serving: 361 Calories, 47G Protein, 28G Carbohydrates, 14G Fat

MIGHTY MUSSEL BROTH

SERVES 2 / PREP TIME: 35 MINUTES / COOK TIME: 40 MINUTES

So easy to prepare.

---

10 OZ MUSSELS (WITHOUT THEIR SHELLS)
OR 2 CUPS MUSSELS WITH SHELLS

1 WHITE ONION. FINELY DICED

1 LEMON, JUICED

1 GARLIC CLOVE, MINCED

1 STALK CELERY, SLICED

1/2 CUP VEG STOCK

1/2 CUP CANNED TOMATOES

2 SLICES WHOLE WHEAT BREAD

1 TSP OLIVE OIL

---

1. Heat the oil in a large pot over a medium heat.
2. Add the onion, garlic and celery and sauté for 4-5 minutes or until starting to soften.
3. Add the tomatoes, stock and lemon juice and bring to the boil.
4. Turn down the heat and allow to simmer for 10 minutes.
5. Add the mussels and cook according to package directions (this will depend on whether they are in their shell or out).
6. The flesh should be vibrant and orange once cooked and the shells will be open.
7. Lightly toast the bread and serve on the side.
8. Dunk in and enjoy!

Per Serving: 447 Calories, 40G Protein, 39G Carbohydrates, 14G Fat

TUNA STEAKS WITH NUTTY GREEN BEANS

SERVES 2 / PREP TIME: 35 MINUTES / COOK TIME: 40 MINUTES

Meaty tuna steaks with crunchy greens.

2X 6OZ TUNA STEAKS, SKINLESS

1 CUP GREEN BEANS

1 TBSP ALMONDS, CRUSHED

1 GARLIC CLOVE, MINCED

1 TBSP OLIVE OIL

1 TBSP BLACK PEPPER CORNS, CRUSHED

1 TSP PARSLEY

---

1. Preheat the oven to its highest setting.
2. Layer the crushed almonds onto a baking tray and roast for 10-15 minutes.
3. Meanwhile, mix the oil with the garlic, pepper and parsley.
4. Marinate the tuna steaks for as long as possible.
5. Steam the green beans over a pot of boiling water for 4-6 minutes.
6. Heat a dry skillet on a medium to high heat.
7. Add the tuna steaks for about 2-3 minutes each side for medium-rare. (Add 1 minute each side for medium and 2 minutes each side for medium well).
8. Remove the tuna and allow to rest.
9. Scatter the roasted almonds over the green beans, season with a little black pepper and serve on the side of the tuna steak. Load up with sweet potato or quinoa if you're looking for extra calories or carbs.

Per Serving: 447 Calories, 40G Protein, 39G Carbohydrates, 14G Fat

CHUNKY COD PARCELS

SERVES 2 / PREP TIME: 35 MINUTES / COOK TIME: 40 MINUTES

Succulent and juicy.

2X COD FILLETS, SKINLESS & DE-BONED	1 TBSP OLIVE OIL
10 PLUM TOMATOES	1 GARLIC CLOVE, HALVED
1 LEMON, HALVED	1/4 RED ONION, SLICED
1/4 CUP OLIVES, PITTED	1 CUP COOKED WHOLE-WHEAT COUSCOUS

1. Preheat oven to 400°f/200°c/Gas Mark 6.
2. Tear off two squares of parchment paper or foil.
3. Add a cod fillet, half the tomatoes, olives, onion, 1 garlic clove onto each sheet.
4. Squeeze the lemon juice over before popping in the wedge.
5. Place in the oven for 15-20 minutes or until cooked through.
6. Serve with couscous and a side of arugula with a drizzle of olive oil and a little black pepper.

Per Serving: 394 Calories, 40G Protein, 49G Carbohydrates, 11G Fat

HADDOCK & KALE CRUMBLE

SERVES 2 / PREP TIME: 35 MINUTES / COOK TIME: 1 HOUR

A lean fish pie.

4X HADDOCK FILLETS, SKINLESS & BONE-LESS

2 CUPS CURLY KALE

1/4 CUP WHOLE-WHEAT BREADCRUMBS

1/2 CUP FROZEN PEAS

2 CUPS RICE MILK/WHOLE MILK

1/4 CUP SESAME SEEDS

1 TSP BLACK PEPPER

1 TSP PARSLEY

---

1. Preheat oven to 400°f/200°c/Gas Mark 6.
2. Add the milk into a pan over a medium to high heat and bring to a simmer.
3. Add the haddock fillets, black pepper and parsley to the pan and lower the heat slightly.
4. Allow to simmer for 20-25 minutes or until cooked through.
5. Meanwhile, add the breadcrumbs and kale to a food processor and blitz together for 30 seconds (you still want a chunky texture).
6. Use a fork to flake the haddock fillets once cooked and return to the milk. Stir in the peas.
7. Into a deep oven dish, add the haddock and milk.
8. Top with the crispy kale mixture and bake in the oven for 25-30 minutes or until golden.

Per Serving: 620 Calories, 66G Protein, 41G Carbohydrates, 25G Fat

SEAFOOD KEBABS & CUCUMBER SALAD

SERVES 2 / PREP TIME: 35 MINUTES / COOK TIME: 40 MINUTES

Get the BBQ ready!

---

6 KING SCALLOPS	1/2 ZUCCHINI
6 WHOLE SHRIMP	2 KEBAB STICKS
1 CUCUMBER	1/2 LIME, JUICED
1 TSP DILL	1 TBSP WHITE WINE VINEGAR

---

1. Preheat the broiler or BBQ to a high heat.
2. Skewer the kebab sticks with the scallops and shrimp.
3. Squeeze the lemon juice over the top of the kebabs.
4. Broil on a lined baking tray for 4-5 minutes or until shrimp and scallops thoroughly cooked through.
5. Peel and slice the cucumber length ways.
6. Mix with the dill and white wine vinegar.
7. Serve the cucumber salad on the side of the kebabs.

Per Serving: 121 Calories, 19G Protein, 8G Carbohydrates, 1G Fat

SOUPS

CARROT, QUINOA & TARRAGON SOUP

SERVES 2 / PREP TIME: 10 MINUTES / COOK TIME: 35 MINUTES

A real zingy soup – great for winter but can be served cooled in the summer too!

2 TBSP OLIVE OIL

1 TSP MUSTARD SEEDS, GROUND

1 TSP FENNEL SEEDS, GROUND

1 TBSP TARRAGON

1 TBSP GINGER, MINCED

1 CUP QUINOA

1 ONION, CHOPPED

6 CARROTS, PEELED & CHOPPED

ZEST AND JUICE OF 1 ORANGE

3 CUPS LOW-SALT VEGETABLE STOCK/ CHICKEN STOCK/WATER

BLACK PEPPER TO TASTE

3 CUPS OF WATER

1. In a pan on a medium heat, add the oil.
2. Once hot, add the seeds for 1 minute.
3. Add the ginger and cook for a further minute.
4. Then add the carrots, onions and the orange juice, cooking for at least 5 minutes or until the vegetables are soft.
5. Add the stock and tarragon and bring to the boil before turning the heat down slightly.
6. Add the quinoa to the pan and simmer for 30 minutes.
7. Allow to cool.
8. Put the mixture in a food processor and puree until smooth (leave some lumps for a chunky soup).
9. Serve with orange zest and black pepper.

Per Serving: 589 Calories, 26G Protein, 71G Carbohydrates, 29G Fat

SPAGHETTI SQUASH & YELLOW LENTIL SOUP

SERVES 2 / PREP TIME: 10 MINUTES / COOK TIME: 45 MINUTES

The lentils add a protein hit to this soup.

---

1 SPAGHETTI SQUASH, PEELED AND CUBED

4 CUPS LOW-SALT VEGETABLE STOCK/ CHICKEN STOCK/WATER

1 TBSP COCONUT OIL

1 ONION, QUARTERED AND SLICED

2 LARGE GARLIC CLOVES, CHOPPED

1 SPRIG OF THYME/1 TBSP DRIED THYME

1 CUP YELLOW LENTILS

1 TSP CURRY POWDER

---

1. Heat oil in a large pan over a medium high heat before sweating the onions and garlic for 3-4 minutes.
2. Add the stock and bring to a boil over a high heat before adding the squash and lentils.
3. Turn down heat and allow to simmer for 25-30 minutes.
4. Now add the rest of the ingredients and simmer for a further 15 minutes or until the squash is tender.
5. Serve hot!

Per Serving: 278 Calories, 19G Protein, 29G Carbohydrates, 15G Fat

RED PEPPER & PINTO BEAN SOUP

SERVES 4 / PREP TIME: 10 MINUTES / COOK TIME: 45 MINUTES

Adding beans to your soup adds a delicious texture and extra goodness!

8 RED BELL PEPPERS, CHOPPED	2 CUP PINTO BEANS, CANNED
1 RED ONION, CHOPPED	2 TBSP OF EXTRA VIRGIN OLIVE OIL
2 GARLIC CLOVES, CHOPPED	1 TSP CUMIN
3 CUPS CHICKEN/VEG STOCK	1 TSP PAPRIKA

1. In a pan on a medium heat, heat the oil then add the onions and peppers, sweating for 5 minutes.
2. Add the garlic cloves, cumin and paprika and saute for 3-4 minutes.
3. Add the broth and allow to boil before turning heat down slightly.
4. Add the pinto beans and simmer for 30 minutes.
5. Remove from the heat and allow to cool slightly.
6. Put the mixture in a food processor and puree until smooth or leave for a chunky soup.
7. Season with black pepper to serve.

Per Serving: 494 Calories, 13G Protein, 26G Carbohydrates, 13G Fat

CHICKEN & LEMONGRASS SOUP

SERVES 4 / PREP TIME: 5 MINUTES / COOK TIME: 40 MINUTES

This chunky soup with asian style broth is a must!

1 TBSP COCONUT OIL

1 TBSP CILANTRO

1 CUP MUSHROOMS

1 FRESH LIME

1 GARLIC CLOVE, MINCED

1 THUMB SIZE PIECE OF MINCED GINGER

1 WHITE ONION, CHOPPED

1/2 CUP PAK CHOI/BOK CHOY

A HANDFUL OF FRESH BASIL LEAVES

1/2 CUP OF CHICKEN BROTH

1/2 CUP OF COCONUT MILK

1 GREEN CHILI, FINELY CHOPPED

2 STEMS OF GREEN ONION, CHOPPED

4X SKINLESS CHICKEN BREASTS, SLICED

1/2 STICK LEMONGRASS, SLICED

1. Crush the lemongrass, cilantro, chili, 1 tbsp oil and basil leaves in a blender or pestle and mortar to form a paste.
2. Heat a large pan/wok with 1 tbsp olive oil on a high heat.
3. Sauté the onions, garlic and ginger until soft.
4. Add the chicken and brown each side.
5. Add the coconut milk and stir. Now add the paste.
6. Slowly add the stock until a broth is formed.
7. Now add the mushrooms, turn down the heat slightly and allow to simmer for 25-30 minutes or until chicken is thoroughly cooked through.
8. Add the bok choy 5 minutes before the end of the cooking time.
9. Serve hot with the green onion sprinkled over the top.

Per Serving: 254 Calories, 33G Protein, 19G Carbohydrates, 12G Fat

CURRIED CHICKPEA & GARLIC SOUP

SERVES 4 / PREP TIME: 10 MINUTES / COOK TIME: 40 MINUTES

Chickpeas are a great way of adding protein to your meal.

2 TBSP COCONUT OIL	1 TSP CUMIN
4 CLOVES GARLIC, MINCED	1 TSP TURMERIC
1/2 CAULIFLOWER, CHOPPED	3 CUPS WATER
2 ONIONS, PEELED AND CHOPPED	1 CUP HOMEMADE CHICKEN STOCK
1 CUP CHICKPEAS, CANNED	1 CUP LOW FAT COCONUT MILK

1. Heat the oil in a large pan over a medium high heat.
2. Add the onions, garlic and cauliflower and sweat for 5-10 minutes (don't let them brown).
3. Add the chickpeas and spices and cook for another 5 minutes.
4. Add the stock and bring to a boil before lowering heat and simmering for 15-20 minutes.
5. Remove from heat and allow to cool before blending in a food processor or liquidizer. Alternatively enjoy chunky and skip step 5.
6. Return to the pan and add the coconut milk, warming through.
7. Serve with a sprinkle of black pepper.

Per Serving: 438 Calories, 17G Protein, 45G Carbohydrates, 24G Fat

NUTMEG, SPINACH & PORK SOUP

SERVES 2 / PREP TIME: 5 MINUTES / COOK TIME: 30 MINUTES

Tasty!

---

1 TBSP EXTRA-VIRGIN OLIVE OIL

1 TBSP GROUND NUTMEG

1 CUP CHICKEN OR VEGE-
TABLE STOCK

6OZ LEAN GROUND PORK

1 ONION, CHOPPED

2 CUPS SPINACH

2 GARLIC CLOVES, MINCED

1 TSP BLACK PEPPER

---

1. In a large pot, add the oil, chopped onion and minced garlic, sautéing for 5 minutes on low heat.
2. Add the pork to the onions and cook for 7-8 minutes or until browned.
3. Add the stock to the pan and bring to a boil on a high heat.
4. Stir in the spinach, reduce heat and simmer for a further 20 minutes or until pork thoroughly cooked through.
5. Allow to cool slightly and add to a food processor until smooth.
6. Season with pepper to serve.

Per Serving: 286 Calories, 22G Protein, 7G Carbohydrates, 27G Fat

WHITE BEAN & MED VEG SOUP

SERVES 2 / PREP TIME: 5 MINUTES / COOK TIME: 30 MINUTES

Hearty, chunky soup.

---

1 TBSP EXTRA-VIRGIN OLIVE OIL	1 ZUCCHINI, FINELY CHOPPED
1 TBSP OREGANO	1 EGGPLANT, FINELY CHOPPED
2 CUPS CHICKEN OR VEGE-TABLE STOCK	1 RED PEPPER, FINELY CHOPPED
1 CUP WHITE BEANS, CANNED	2 GARLIC CLOVES, MINCED
1 ONION, CHOPPED	1 TSP BLACK PEPPER

---

1. In a large pot, add the oil, chopped onion and minced garlic, sautéing for 5 minutes on low heat.
2. Add the other vegetables to the onions and cook for 7-8 minutes or until browned.
3. Add the stock to the pan and bring to a boil on a high heat.
4. Stir in the herbs and beans, reduce heat and simmer for a further 20 minutes or until thoroughly cooked through.
5. Season with pepper to serve.

Per Serving: 326 Calories, 20G Protein, 38G Carbohydrates, 14G Fat

HEALTHY VEGETABLE STOCK

SERVES 2 / PREP TIME: 10 MINUTES / COOK TIME: 35 MINUTES

Use as a healthy alternative to shop bought stocks.

2 ONIONS	1 TBSP EXTRA VIRGIN OLIVE OIL
3 CARROTS	1 BAY LEAF
3 CELERY STALKS	1 TBSP THYME
1 GARLIC CLOVE	1 TBSP PARSLEY
	1 TSP BLACK PEPPERCORNS

1. Peel and chop vegetables and soak in warm water.
2. Heat the oil in a large pot over a medium heat and add the vegetables, garlic, herbs and peppercorns, cooking for 5 minutes.
3. Fill up the pot with boiling water.
4. Turn up the heat and bring to the boil - allow to simmer for 25 minutes.
5. Strain stock and use immediately or allow to cool and refrigerate for 2-3 days or freeze for 3-4 weeks in a sealed container.

Per Serving: 5 Calories, 1G Protein, 1G Carbohydrates, 0G Fat

LEAN CHICKEN STOCK

SERVES 2 / PREP TIME: 10 MINUTES / COOK TIME: 4 HOURS

Use as a healthy alternative to shop bought stocks.

---

1 WHOLE ROASTING CHICKEN {AROUND 4-5LBS}

3 CARROTS, SOAKED IN WARM WATER

2 MEDIUM ONIONS

4 GARLIC CLOVES, CRUSHED

2 BAY LEAVES

3 STALKS OF CELERY, SOAKED IN WARM WATER

1 TBSP EACH DRIED ROSEMARY, THYME, PEPPER, TURMERIC

1 TBSP WHITE WINE VINEGAR

11-12 CUPS WATER

---

1. Rinse off your chicken and place in a large saucepan or soup pan (remove giblets but don't waste them; add them in to your stock bowl!)
2. Chop your vegetables into large chunks (quarters at the smallest). Leave the skins on as they add to the taste and the nutrients - add to the pan.
3. Add the herbs, spices and pepper to the pan.
4. Fill your pan with water so that the chicken and vegetables are completely covered.
5. Turn stove on high and bring to boiling point before reducing the heat and allowing the stock to simmer for 3-4 hours.
6. Check at intervals and top up with water if the ingredients become uncovered.
7. Take off the heat and carefully remove the chicken, placing to one side.
8. You now need to strain the liquid from the stockpot into another bowl using a sieve to get rid of all the lumpy bits.
9. Leave the stock and chicken to cool.
10. Once cool, tear or cut the meat from the bones.
11. Once the stock has cooled to room temperature, add to a sealed container and keep in the fridge.
12. Save the chicken for a delicious salad or to add back into the stock to make a chunky chicken soup.
13. The stock can be kept for 3 days in the fridge/3 months in freezer in an airtight Tupperware box or Kilner jar - just skim off the fat when ready to use.

Per Serving: 71 Calories, 9G Protein, 2G Carbohydrates, 7G Fat

SIDES, SALADS AND SNACKS

PEAR & PECAN CHIPS

SERVES 4 / PREP TIME: 5 MINUTES / COOK TIME: 30 MINUTES

A delicious snack that will satisfy your sweet cravings!

---

4 PEARS, PEELED AND THINLY SLICED   1/4 CUP OF PECAN PIECES FOR TOPPING

1 TBSP CINNAMON

---

1. Preheat oven to 190°C/375°F/Gas Mark 5.
2. Layer the pear slices in a thin layer on a baking tray.
3. Dust with the cinnamon and top with pecan pieces.
4. Bake for 20-30 minutes or until crispy.

Per Serving: 149 Calories, 2G Protein, 28G Carbohydrates, 5G Fat

MIXED SEED TOPPER

SERVES 4 / PREP TIME: 5 MINUTES / COOK TIME: 15 MINUTES

Energy boosting bites – great as a topping for cereals or soups, or as a quick pick me up throughout the day!

1/4 CUP PUMPKIN SEEDS	1 TSP PAPRIKA
1/4 CUP SUNFLOWER SEEDS	1 TSP HONEY
1 TBSP EXTRA VIRGIN OLIVE OIL	1 TSP DRIED THYME

1. Preheat oven to 375°F/190 °C/Gas Mark 5.
2. Layer the seeds on a baking tray.
3. Combine the rest of the ingredients together and coat the seeds evenly.
4. Bake for 15 minutes and then transfer to a sealable container to snack on or sprinkle on your oats or salads.

Per Serving: 99 Calories, 3G Protein, 5G Carbohydrates, 8G Fat

BLUEBERRY ENERGY BURST

SERVES 4 / PREP TIME: 5 MINUTES / COOK TIME: 20 MINUTES

An energizing snack.

---

1 CUP TOASTED PECANS	1/2 CUP BLUEBERRIES
1 TBSP RAW HONEY	1 CUP GRANOLA

---

1. Preheat oven to 350°F/170 °C/Gas Mark 4.
2. Spread the walnuts across a baking sheet.
3. Bake for five minutes and then add the blueberries and granola and toss with a fork.
4. Drizzle honey on top and toss again to coat before baking in oven for 10-15 minutes.
5. Remove to cool.
6. Serve.

Per Serving: 316 Calories, 6G Protein, 26G Carbohydrates, 23G Fat

PARSNIP & RUTABAGA CHIPS

SERVES 2 / PREP TIME: 5 MINUTES / COOK TIME: 50 MINUTES

A healthy alternative to the ones you get in a bag!

---

2 PARSNIPS, PEELED AND SLICED

1 RUTABAGA, PEELED & SLICED

1 TBSP EXTRA VIRGIN OLIVE OIL

1 TSP BLACK PEPPER

1 TSP THYME

1 TSP CHILI FLAKES

---

1. Heat oven to 375°f/190°c/Gas Mark 5.
2. Grease a baking tray with the olive oil.
3. Add parsnip and rutabaga slices in a thin layer.
4. Dust over thyme and chili flakes and toss to coat.
5. Bake for 40-50 minutes (turning half way through to ensure even crispiness!)

Per Serving: 160 Calories, 6G Protein, 24G Carbohydrates, 7G Fat

HOMEMADE SWEET POTATO FRIES

SERVES 2 / PREP TIME: 5 MINUTES / COOK TIME: 30 MINUTES

Stack these up with your favorite dish.

---

2 LARGE SWEET POTATOES, CUT INTO THIN STRIPS

1 TSP OF TARRAGON

1 TSP ROSEMARY

1 TBSP OF EXTRA VIRGIN OLIVE OIL

1 TBSP OF BLACK PEPPER

---

1. Preheat oven to 375°F/190 °C/Gas Mark 5.
2. Add the sweet potato strips into a large bowl.
3. Drizzle with some olive oil.
4. Sprinkle the rest of the ingredients over the top.
5. Toss together gently to evenly coat the potatoes.
6. Get a baking sheet and arrange the coated potatoes into a thin layer.
7. Bake for around 30 minutes or until cooked through.
8. Serve.

Per Serving: 236 Calories, 2G Protein, 38G Carbohydrates, 8G Fat

RED PEPPER HUMMUS

SERVES 4 /   PREP TIME: 10 MINUTES / COOK TIME: NA

A delicious protein packed dip for your favorite vegetables.

FOR THE HUMMUS:

1 CAN OF CHICKPEAS

2 CLOVES OF GARLIC, MINCED

1 TBSP TAHINI PASTE

4 TBSP EXTRA VIRGIN OLIVE OIL

1 TSP GROUND CUMIN

1 RED PEPPER, FINELY DICED

1 TSP SALT

1 LEMON, JUICED

---

1. Take all of the ingredients for the hummus and add to a food processor until smooth.
2. Serve!

Per Serving: 192 Calories, 7G Protein, 25G Carbohydrates, 29G Fat

POWERFUL PUMPKIN MASH

SERVES 4 / PREP TIME: 5 MINUTES / COOK TIME: 30 MINUTES

Slow releasing carbs to keep you training longer.

FLESH OF 1 PUMPKIN

1/2 SWEDE, CHOPPED

3 GARLIC CLOVES, CHOPPED

1/4 CUP PARSLEY, FINELY CHOPPED

1 TBSP EXTRA VIRGIN OLIVE OIL

A PINCH OF BLACK PEPPER

2 TBSP LOW FAT GREEK YOGURT

---

1. Add the pumpkin, swede and garlic to a large pan of water, bring to the boil, and then lower the heat and simmer for 30 minutes or until soft.
2. Drain.
3. Add the parsley and olive oil and season with pepper.
4. Mash with a potato masher.
5. Stir in the low fat Greek yogurt.
6. Serve and enjoy!

Per Serving: 50 Calories, 1G Protein, 4G Carbohydrates, 4G Fat

LATIN RICE

SERVES 2 / PREP TIME: 5 MINUTES / COOK TIME: 25 MINUTES

The citrus flavors blend perfectly with the black beans.

1/2 CUP BLACK BEANS, CANNED

2 CUPS HOMEMADE CHICKEN STOCK

1 CUP UNCOOKED BROWN RICE

1 TBSP EXTRA VIRGIN OLIVE OIL

1 RED ONION, CHOPPED

1 TBSP CILANTRO, CHOPPED

1 RED PEPPER, FINELY DICED

1 LIME, ZEST AND JUICE

---

1. Add the stock and brown rice into a saucepan and boil on a high heat.
2. Reduce the heat, add the beans and simmer for 25 minutes until rice is cooked and the liquid is nearly absorbed.
3. Meanwhile, heat the oil in a skillet on a medium heat and sauté the onion until soft.
4. Add the peppers and cook for another 10 minutes.
5. Stir the onions and peppers into the rice and beans and then squeeze in the lime juice and top with cilantro and lime zest.

Per Serving: 321 Calories, 16G Protein, 41G Carbohydrates, 15G Fat

NUTTY GREEN BEANS & BROCCOLI

SERVES 4 / PREP TIME: 5 MINUTES / COOK TIME: 25 MINUTES

This is a simple and flavorsome salad.

1/2 CUP PEANUTS	1 TSP PEPPER
1/2 CUP WATER	2 CUPS BROCCOLI, SLICED
1 TBSP PEANUT OIL	2 CUPS GREEN BEANS
1 TBSP LOW SODIUM SOY SAUCE	

---

1. Preheat oven to the highest heat.
2. Layer the peanuts onto a dry baking tray and add to the oven for 5-10 minutes or until nuts start to brown. Turn whilst cooking to ensure even browning.
3. Remove to cool.
4. Meanwhile boil a pan of water on a medium heat and add the broccoli.
5. Cook on a simmer for 5-10 minutes or until cooked through. Add the green beans in the last 7-8 minutes.
6. Drain and place to one side.
7. Once cool, crush the peanuts on a wooden chopping board or similar, using a sharp knife.
8. Mix the peanut oil with the soy sauce and dress the broccoli and green beans.
9. Sprinkle with peanuts to serve.

Per Serving: 146 Calories, 7G Protein, 5G Carbohydrates, 12G Fat

TURKEY & TABBOULEH SALAD

SERVES 2 / PREP TIME: 35 MINUTES / COOK TIME: NA

A variation of the traditional tabbouleh salad, this version features goats' cheese for a tasty twist.

2X TURKEY BREAST

8 CHERRY TOMATOES, HALVED

1 LEMON, JUICED

2 TBSP OF THYME

1 TSP OF BLACK PEPPER

1 RED ONION, DICED

1/4 CUP TABBOULEH, SPIRALYZED

1 CUP SPINACH LEAVES

1 TBSP OLIVE OIL

1/2 CUCUMBER, DICED

1. Combine lemon juice, olive oil, tabbouleh, spinach, cucumber, turkey, tomatoes, red onion, pepper and thyme in a large bowl.
2. Gently toss to mix well and serve.

Per Serving: 317 Calories, 40G Protein, 20G Carbohydrates, 9G Fat

SPINACH PESTO & CRUDITES

SERVES 5 / PREP TIME: 5 MINUTES / COOK TIME: NA

Delicious friendly pesto!

1/2 CUP FRESH BASIL

1 CUP FRESH SPINACH

1 TSP BLACK PEPPER

1/4 CUP EXTRA VIRGIN OLIVE OIL

2 GARLIC CLOVES AS ALTERNATIVE)

1 LEMON, JUICED

1 CARROT, PEELED & SLICED

1 STICK OF CELERY, SLICED

---

1. Blend all ingredients in a food processor or a blender to reach required texture - chunky for a rustic feel or smooth as a dressing.
2. Store in an airtight container in the fridge for 3-4 days.
3. Serve with the fresh vegetables to dip in!

Per Serving: 117 Calories, 4G Protein, 7G Carbohydrates, 4G Fat

GOATS' CHEESE, ENDIVE & POMEGRANATE SALAD

SERVES 2 / PREP TIME: 5 MINUTES / COOK TIME: 25 MINUTES

The aniseed taste of the endive blends perfectly with the sweet burst of pomegranate seeds.

1/2 CUP CRUMBLED GOATS' CHEESE

1 ENDIVE PLANT, WASHED

1 TBSP RED WINE VINEGAR

3 TBSP OLIVE OIL

1 CUP WATERCRESS (STALKS REMOVED)

1 TSP SALT

1 TSP PEPPER

---

1. Heat a dry griddle pan over a medium to high heat.
2. Add the endive leaves and griddle for 3-4 minutes on each side. Remove.
3. Slice the pomegranate in half and use a spoon to scoop out the seeds. Retain the seeds.
4. In a salad bowl, add the watercress and pomegranate seeds.
5. Whisk together the olive oil, vinegar, salt and pepper together to make the dressing. Drizzle the dressing over the salad along with the crumbled cheese and endive leaves.
6. Toss and serve ASAP.

Per Serving: 270 Calories, 5G Protein, 3G Carbohydrates, 25G Fat

CUCUMBER, POPPY SEED & ARUGULA SALAD

SERVES 2 / PREP TIME: 5 MINUTES / COOK TIME: 25 MINUTES

Fresh green salad with a crunchy top.

---

2 CUCUMBERS, SPIRALYZED	1 TBSP RAW HONEY
1 TBSP OF OLIVE OIL	1 TBSP POPPY SEEDS
1 CUP OF ARUGULA	1 CRUSHED GARLIC CLOVE
1 TBSP LEMON JUICE	PINCH OF SALT
	PINCH OF PEPPER

---

1. Add all the ingredients to a large salad bowl and toss thoroughly.
2. Sprinkle some salt and pepper over the salad to finish.

Per Serving: 111 Calories, 1G Protein, 12G Carbohydrates, 7G Fat

ZUCCHINI, BULGHAR WHEAT AND EGGPLANT SALAD

SERVES 2 / PREP TIME: 5 MINUTES / COOK TIME: 25 MINUTES

A chunky salad on the side.

---

2 CUPS BULGHAR WHEAT, COOKED

5 SUN DRIED TOMATOES

1 ZUCCHINI, SLICED

1 EGGPLANT, SLICED

2 TBSP OLIVE OIL

2 DICED RED PEPPERS

1/2 CUP SPINACH LEAVES

PINCH OF SALT

PINCH OF PEPPER

---

1. Pre heat a griddle pan over a high heat and add the eggplant slices for 10 minutes, turning over half way through, until lightly charred.
2. Remove from the pan and place to one side.
3. Now add a little live oil and the zucchini slices. Repeat above.
4. In a bowl, mix the bulghar wheat, sun-dried tomatoes and a little oil from the jar together.
5. Add the eggplant, red peppers, zucchini, salt and pepper and spinach leaves.
6. Toss together and serve.

Per Serving: 291 Calories, 11G Protein, 60G Carbohydrates, 15G Fat

BUTTER BEAN, TOMATO & SPRING ONION SALAD

SERVES 2 / PREP TIME: 5 MINUTES / COOK TIME: 25 MINUTES

Light and refreshing!

1/2 CUP BUTTER BEANS	10 CHERRY TOMATOES, SLICED
2 TBSP CHOPPED SPRING ONIONS	1 CUP WATERCRESS
2 TBSP OLIVE OIL	PINCH OF SALT
1 TBSP CHOPPED PARSLEY	PINCH OF PEPPER
2 TBSP OF WHITE WINE VINEGAR	

---

1. Add all the ingredients to a large salad bowl and toss thoroughly.
2. Sprinkle salt and pepper over the salad to finish.

Per Serving: 194 Calories, 3G Protein, 15G Carbohydrates, 12G Fat

CRAB & ARUGULA SALAD

SERVES 2 / PREP TIME: 5 MINUTES / COOK TIME: 25 MINUTES

A chunky salad on the side.

6OZ CRAB MEAT

1 CUP ARUGULA

2 TBSP OF OLIVE OIL

1/2 CUP LOW FAT GREEK YOGURT

10 HALVED CHERRY TOMATOES

JUICE OF 1 LEMON

PINCH OF SALT

PINCH OF PEPPER

---

1. Get a small bowl and add the crab meat, lemon juice and yogurt.
2. Mix well.
3. Season with salt and pepper and leave to one side.
4. In a salad bowl, add the arugula, tomatoes and avocado.
5. Drizzle with the olive oil and then toss thoroughly.
6. Stir through the crab meat mixture and enjoy.

Per Serving: 207 Calories, 12G Protein, 12G Carbohydrates, 14G Fat

SHAKES, DRINKS AND DESSERTS

CHOCOLATE & BERRY SHAKE

SERVES 2 / PREP TIME: 5 MINUTES / COOK TIME: NA

Delicious pre or post workout shake.

---

2 SCOOPS CHOCOLATE PROTEIN POWDER

1/8 CUP MIXED BERRIES (FROZEN)

1 TSP GOJI BERRIES

1/8 CUP SPINACH

1/2 CUP ALMOND MILK

---

1. Add all ingredients to a blender until smooth.
2. Serve.

Per Serving: 214 Calories, 28G Protein, 19G Carbohydrates, 4G Fat

BRILLIANT BANANA SHAKE

SERVES 2 / PREP TIME: 5 MINUTES / COOK TIME: NA MINUTES

Tropical smoothie.

---

1 BANANA

1/8 CUP KALE

1/2 APPLE, SLICED

1 TSP FLAXSEED

1/2 CUP WATER

2 SCOOPS VANILLA PROTEIN POWDER

---

1. Add all ingredients to a blender until smooth.
2. Serve.

Per Serving: 216 Calories, 25G Protein, 21G Carbohydrates, 5G Fat

TANGERINE TWIST

SERVES 2 / PREP TIME: 5 MINUTES / COOK TIME: 25 MINUTES

Packed with Vitamin C!

---

5 TANGERINES

1/8 CUP SPINACH

ICECUBES

1/2 CUP WATER

1 TSP BASIL LEAVES

---

1. Blend all ingredients until smooth.
2. Serve.

Per Serving: 121 Calories, 4G Protein, 27G Carbohydrates, 1G Fat

POWER PROTEIN SHAKE

SERVES 1 / PREP TIME: 5 MINUTES / COOK TIME: NA MINUTES

Healthy fats and protein make this a between meal fave!

---

2 TBSP GREEK YOGURT

1 SCOOP ROLLED OATS

1 TBSP ALMONDS

1 TSP RAW HONEY

1 SCOOP VANILLA PROTEIN

1/8 CUP FROZEN RASPBERRIES

---

1. Blend all ingredients until smooth.
2. Serve.

Per Serving: 440 Calories, 4G Protein, 33G Carbohydrates, 10G Fat

IMMUNE BOOST

SERVES 1 / PREP TIME: 5 MINUTES / COOK TIME: NA

Beat the common cold with this tasty juice.

---

1 ORANGE, JUICED

2 PEACHES, PEELED AND SLICED

1/4 CARROT, PEELED AND SLICED

1/2 CUP WATER

1 TBSP GOJI BERRIES

---

1. Blend all ingredients until smooth.
2. Serve.

Per Serving: 229 Calories, 3G Protein, 30G Carbohydrates, 1G Fat

LEMON BOOST

SERVES 1 / PREP TIME: 5 MINUTES / COOK TIME: NA

A refreshing drink!

---

2 TBSP LEMON JUICE

2 TBSP STEVIA

4 PASTEURIZED LIQUID EGG WHITES

1 TSP CINNAMON

---

1. Combine all ingredients in a blender until smooth.
2. Garnish with a slice of lemon.

Per Serving: 79 Calories, 14G Protein, 4G Carbohydrates, 1G Fat

GINGER & LEMON GREEN ICED-TEA

SERVES 2 / PREP TIME: 5 MINUTES / COOK TIME: NA

Ditch the latte for this energizing drink!

---

2 CUPS CONCENTRATED GREEN OR MACHA
TEA, SERVED HOT

1 LEMON, CUT INTO WEDGES

1/4 CUP CRYSTALLIZED GINGER, CHOPPED
INTO FINE PIECES

---

1. Get a glass container and mix the tea with the ginger and then cover and chill for 3 hours.
2. Strain and pour into serving glasses on top of ice if you wish.
3. Garnish with a wedge of lemon to serve.

Per Serving: 0 Calories, 0G Protein, 0G Carbohydrates, 0G Fat

BANANA & PEANUT MILKSHAKE

SERVES 1 / PREP TIME: 5 MINUTES / COOK TIME: NA

A rich shake to fill up on between meals.

---

2 TBSP PEANUT BUTTER (NO ADDED SUGAR OR SALT)

1 BANANA

2 CUPS ALMOND MILK

1 TSP RAW HONEY

2 SCOOPS OF VANILLA PROTEIN POWDER

---

1. Blend all ingredients until smooth.
2. Serve.

Per Serving: 642 Calories, 48G Protein, 48G Carbohydrates, 25G Fat

YOGURT SHAKE

SERVES 2 / PREP TIME: 5 MINUTES / COOK TIME: NA

A refreshing drink!

---

1 CUP GREEK YOGURT

1 TBSP RAW HONEY

1/2 CUP ROLLED OATS

1 TBSP COCONUT OIL

1 SCOOP OF VANILLA PROTEIN POWDER

---

1. Combine all ingredients in a blender until smooth.

Per Serving: 402 Calories, 23G Protein, 23G Carbohydrates, 23G Fat

CRUNCHY APPLE PIE

SERVES 4 / PREP TIME: 5 MINUTES / COOK TIME: 1 HOUR

Oven baked hearty dessert.

---

2 CUPS COOKING APPLES, PEELED AND SLICED

2 WHOLE CLOVES

1 TSP CINNAMON

1 CUP WHOLE-WHEAT BREADCRUMBS

1/4 CUP HAZELNUTS, CRUSHED

1 TBSP COCONUT OIL

---

1. Preheat the oven to 190°C/375°F/Gas Mark 5.
2. Boil a pot of water over a high heat and add the apples, cloves and cinnamon.
3. Turn down the heat slightly and allow to cook for 30-35 minutes or until very soft.
4. Drain and add apples to the bottom of an oven dish.
5. Blitz up the breadcrumbs and hazelnuts and add coconut oil to combine.
6. Top the apples with this mixture and place in the oven to bake for 20-30 minutes or until golden brown.

Per Serving: 137 Calories, 2G Protein, 20G Carbohydrates, 6G Fat

STRAWBERRY MOUSSE

SERVES 3 / PREP TIME: 5 MINUTES / COOK TIME: NA

Try mixing this up for a guilt-free dessert.

---

2 CUPS SILKEN EXTRA FIRM TOFU

2 TBSP SOY MILK

3 SCOOPS STRAWBERRY FLAVOURED
PROTEIN POWDER

1/2 CUP FRESH STRAWBERRIES

---

1. Blend the tofu and milk until smooth (you can use water here instead if you wish).
2. Now add the protein powder until smooth.
3. Add the mousse into serving cups and cover and refrigerate for 4-5 hours.
4. Enjoy with fresh strawberries.

Per Serving: 236 Calories, 35G Protein, 9G Carbohydrates, 8G Fat

PECAN & DARK CHOCOLATE CHIP COOKIES

SERVES 6 / PREP TIME: 10 MINUTES / COOK TIME: 10 MINUTES

Wholegrain cookies without the sin.

1 CUP PECANS	1/4 CUP STEVIA
1 CUP GROUND FLAX MEAL	1 FREE RANGE EGG
2 CUPS WHOLEGRAIN ROLLED OATS	1/4 CUP COCONUT OIL
1 TSP NUTMEG	1 TSP VANILLA EXTRACT
1/2 CUP WHOLE WHEAT FLOUR	1 CUP DARK CHOCOLATE CHIPS
1 TSP BAKING SODA	1/2 CUP BLUEBERRIES
	1/2 CUP WHOLE ALMOND BUTTER

1. Preheat the oven to 190°C/375°F/Gas Mark 5.
2. Line a baking dish with parchment paper.
3. Grind the walnuts in a blender to make flour.
4. Add all of the other ingredients (except for the almond butter, blueberries and chocolate chips) and process.
5. Add mixture to a bowl and then fold in the chocolate chips and blueberries.
6. Mix the flour mixture into the almond butter until a sticky dough is formed.
7. Use a tablespoon to spoon mini cookie shapes onto your baking tray and bake for 9 minutes before placing them on a wire rack to cool.

Per Serving: 346 Calories, 8G Protein, 28G Carbohydrates, 23G Fat

RASPBERRY & VANILLA MUFFINS

SERVES 4 / PREP TIME: 5 MINUTES / COOK TIME: 20 MINUTES

Bake these up and enjoy!

---

3 EGG WHITES

1/10 CUP CHICKPEA FLOUR

1 TBSP COCONUT FLOUR

1 TSP OF BAKING POWDER

1 TBSP NUTMEG, GRATED

1 TSP VANILLA EXTRACT

1 TSP STEVIA

1/2 CUP FRESH RASPBERRIES

---

1. Pre-heat the oven to 325°F/170 °C/Gas Mark 3.
2. Mix all of the ingredients in a mixing bowl.
3. Divide the batter into 4 and spoon into a muffin tin.
4. Bake in the oven for 15-20 minutes or until cooked through.
5. Your knife should pull out clean from the middle of the muffins once done.
6. Allow to cool on a wired rack before serving.

Per Serving: 36 Calories, 4G Protein, 4G Carbohydrates, 1G Fat

RAISIN & COCONUT BOOSTERS

SERVES 4 / PREP TIME: 5 MINUTES / COOK TIME: NA

Snack on these.

---

1 CUP SUN-DRIED RAISINS, FINELY CHOPPED

1/2 CUP WALNUTS, FINELY CHOPPED

1/2 CUP DESICCATED COCONUT

1 TBSP HONEY

---

1. Mix the ingredients together to form a sticky dough.
2. Shape into bite size balls with the palms of your hands.
3. Cover and refrigerate for at least 2 hours to set.
4. Serve or wrap for later.

Per Serving: 241 Calories, 6G Protein, 35G Carbohydrates, 10G Fat

VANILLA PANCAKES & APRICOTS

SERVES 2 / PREP TIME: 5 MINUTES / COOK TIME: 10 MINUTES

Amazing!

---

2 SCOOPS VANILLA PROTEIN POWDER	1 TBSP COCONUT OIL
2 FREE RANGE EGG WHITES	1 CUP GREEK YOGURT
2 TBSP OF RAW COCONUT FLOUR	2 APRICOTS, SLICED
	1 TSP NUTMEG

---

1. Get a bowl and combine all the ingredients.
2. Mix well to form a thick batter.
3. Heat a skillet on a medium heat and add the coconut oil.
4. Pour half the mixture into the centre of the pan to form a pancake and cook through for 3-4 minutes on each side.
5. Serve with the peach slices and a dusting of nutmeg.

Per Serving: 345 Calories, 39G Protein, 25G Carbohydrates, 10G Fat

CONVERSION TABLES

Volume

Imperial	Metric
1 tbsp	15ml
2 fl oz	55 ml
3 fl oz	75 ml
5 fl oz (¼ pint)	150 ml
10 fl oz (½ pint)	275 ml
1 pint	570 ml
1 ¼ pints	725 ml
1 ¾ pints	1 litre
2 pints	1.2 litres
2½ pints	1.5 litres
4 pints	2.25 litres

Oven temperatures

Gas Mark	Fahrenheit	Celsius
1/4	225	110
1/2	250	130
1	275	140
2	300	150
3	325	170
4	350	180
5	375	190
6	400	200
7	425	220
8	450	230
9	475	240

Weight

Imperial	Metric
½ oz	10 g
¾ oz	20 g
1 oz	25 g
1½ oz	40 g
2 oz	50 g
2½ oz	60 g
3 oz	75 g
4 oz	110 g
4½ oz	125 g
5 oz	150 g
6 oz	175 g
7 oz	200 g
8 oz	225 g
9 oz	250 g
10 oz	275 g
12 oz	350 g

REFERENCES

Schoenfeld, Brad, Alan Aragon, and James W. Krieger. "The Effect of Protein Timing on Muscle Strength and Hypertrophy: A Meta-analysis." J Int Soc Sports Nutr Journal of the International Society of Sports Nutrition 10, no. 1 (2013): 53. doi:10.1186/1550-2783-10-53.

Kumar, V., P. Atherton, K. Smith, and M. J. Rennie. "Human Muscle Protein Synthesis and Breakdown during and after Exercise." Journal of Applied Physiology 106, no. 6 (2009): 2026-039. doi:10.1152/japplphysiol.91481.2008.

Langley-Evans, Simon. "Keith N. Frayn Metabolic Regulation: A Human Perspective, 2nd Ed. Oxford, UK: Blackwell Publishing 2003. P. 339. £24.99 (paperback). ISBN 0-632-06384-X." BJN British Journal of Nutrition 92, no. 06 (2004): 1013. doi:10.1079/bjn20041232.

Rickli, Jonas. "Bodybuilding." Grenzbereiche Der Sportmedizin, 1990, 159-76. doi:10.1007/978-3-642-75429-6_11.

"Understanding Bodybuilding." Science Signaling 2004, no. 239 (2004). doi:10.1126/stke.2392004tw227.

Lacovara, Paul Dominick. Bodybuilding. 2002.

Gilman, Sander L. Diets and Dieting: A Cultural Encyclopedia. New York: Routledge, 2008.

Jacobs, Peter, and Lucille Wood. Macronutrients. St. Louis, MO: Mosby, 2004.

INDEX

A

Alcohol 12
Apple
  Crunchy Apple Pie 176
Apricot
  Vanilla Pancakes & Apricots 181
Arugula
  Crab & Arugula Salad 165
  Cucumber, Poppy Seed & Arugula Salad 162
Asparagus
  Aesthetic Asparagus & Beetroot Tart 105
Avocado
  Eggs In Avocados! 34
  Salmon Burgers With Avocado 122

B

Banana
  Banana & Hazelnut Oatmeal 40
  Banana & Peanut Milkshake 174
  Bodybuilder's Banana Pancakes 47
  Brilliant Banana Shake 168
Beef
  Barbell Beef Curry 80
  Beef Chili Con Carne 92
  Beef & Pearl Barley Casserole 86
  Bodybuilding Beef Stew 75
  Chili Beef In Lettuce Tortillas 85
  Chili Beef & Mango Salsa 81
  Chunky Chinese Stir Fry 82
  Classic Steak, Mushroom & Eggs 45
  Eggplant & Sweet Potato Lasagne 87
  Lean Beef Stroganoff 84
  Lemongrass & Chili Beef 77
  Mix 'N' Match Beef Burger 73
  Muscle-Friendly Lasagne 79
  Muscle Meatball & Celeriac Spaghetti 76
  Roasted Rump & Root Veg 72
  Slow Cooked Spicy Steak & Beans 90
  Steak, Egg & Mushroom Frenzy 88
  Sweet Potato Cottage Pie 91
Bell Peppers

  Mighty Stuffed Peppers 62
  Red Pepper & Pinto Bean Soup 142
  Spanish Paella 107
  White Bean & Med Veg Soup 146
Blueberry
  Blueberry Energy Burst 152
Broccoli
  Nutty Green Beans & Broccoli 158
Brown rice
  Calamari & Shrimp Paella 114
  Cod, Pea & Spinach Risotto 118
  Red Thai Curry With Duck 89
  Slow Cooked Spicy Steak & Beans 90
Brown Rice
  Chinese Tempah Stir Fry 104
  Latin Rice 157
  Lean Beef Stroganoff 84
Buckwheat
  Brawny Buckwheat Breakfast Granola 31
Butter Bean
  Butter Bean, Tomato & Spring Onion Salad 164

C

Calamari
  Calamari & Shrimp Paella 114
Calories 8
Carbohydrates 10
Carrot
  Carrot Noodles & Cilantro Chicken 58
  Carrot, Quinoa & Tarragon Soup 140
  Chicken With Homemade Slaw 64
  Healthy Vegetable Stock 147
  Immune Boost 171
  Moroccan Lamb Tagine 83
  Powerful Pork & Speedy Sauerkraut 78
Cheese
  Creamy Walnut Penne 102
Chicken
  Artichoke & Tomato Chicken Bake 50
  Cajun Chicken 51
  Carrot Noodles & Cilantro Chicken 58

  Cheeky Chicken Curry 65
  Chicken Burgers & Guacamole 52
  Chicken & Lemongrass Soup 143
  Chicken With Homemade Slaw 64
  Epic Egg Muffins 38
  Lean Chicken Stock 148
  Lemon Chicken With Swede & Kale Puree 66
  Mediterranean Chicken & Eggplant 60
  Mighty Stuffed Peppers 62
  Nourishing Nutty Noodles 56
  Oven-Bakes Chicken Thighs 55
  Powerful Pesto Chicken 59
  Tandoori Style Chicken Drumsticks 69
  Tomato, Mozzarella & Basil Chicken 67
Chickpea
  Curried Chickpea & Garlic Soup 144
  Heavy Haddock & Bean Stew 123
  Red Pepper Hummus 155
  Spiced Cauliflower & Chickpea Curry 100
Coconut
  Raisin & Coconut Boosters 180
Cod
  Chunky Cod Parcels 136
  Cod, Pea & Spinach Risotto 118
  Thai Training Broth 132
Couscous
  Turkey Meatballs & Couscous 70
Crab
  Crab & Arugula Salad 165
Cranberries
  Turkey & Cranberry Sauce 68

D

Diet and nutrition 7
Duck
  Divine Duck Breasts 53
  Red Thai Curry With Duck 89

E

Eggplant
  Eggplant & Sweet Potato Lasagne

87
White Bean & Med Veg Soup 146
Zucchini, Bulghar Wheat And Eggplant Salad 163
Eggs
Aesthetic Asparagus & Beetroot Tart 105
Bodybuilder's Banana Pancakes 47
Classic Steak, Mushroom & Eggs 45
Eggs In Avocados! 34
Epic Egg Muffins 38
Get-Fit Frittata 33
Kino Kedgeree 108
Lemon Boost 172
Pumpin' Pumpkin Pancakes 46
Raspberry & Vanilla Muffins 179
Scallion & Goats Cheese Pancakes 110
Score-board scotch eggs 37
Steak, Egg & Mushroom Frenzy 88
Strengthening Spinach Scramble 43
Sweet Potato Pancakes 44
Terrific Tuna Nicoise 125
Turkey Bacon Omelette 39
Vanilla Pancakes & Apricots 181
Workout Waffles 42

F

Fats 11

G

Garlic & Lemon Shrimp Linguine 133
Glycemic index 11
Goats' Cheese
Goats' Cheese, Endive & Pomegranate Salad 161
Greek Yogurt
Power Protein Shake 170
Vanilla Pancakes & Apricots 181
Yogurt Shake 175
Green Tea
Ginger & Lemon Green Iced-Tea 173

H

Haddock
Haddock & Kale Crumble 137
Heavy Haddock & Bean Stew 123
Halibut
Heavy Haddock & Bean Stew 124
Halloumi
Toasted Sesame & Peanut Tofu 98

L

Lamb
Fit Lamb Steaks With Tzatziki 74
Moroccan Lamb Tagine 83
Langoustine
Langoustine & Sweet Potato Fries 120
Lentils
Mexican Beans & Quinoa 95
Spaghetti Squash & Yellow Lentil Soup 141
Spanish Paella 107

M

Mahi-Mahi
Ginger & Honey Mahi-Mahi With Orange Salad 127
Mixed Berries
Chocolate & Berry Shake 167
Monkfish 125
Sesame Monkfish & Fruit Salsa 126
Mushrooms
Chicken & Lemongrass Soup 143
Garlic Stuffed Mushrooms 101
Mussel
Mighty Mussel Broth 134

N

Noodles
Chunky Chinese Stir Fry 82
Coconut Shrimp & Noodles 130
Nourishing Nutty Noodles 56
Thai Training Broth 132
Nuts
Creamy walnut penne 102
Pumpkin & Pine Nut Casserole 103

P

Parsnip
Parsnip & Rutabaga Chips 153
Pasta
Creamy Walnut Penne 102
Pears
Pear & Pecan Chips 150
Pork
Nutmeg, Spinach & Pork Soup

145
Powerful Pork & Speedy Sauerkraut 78
Sizzling Sausage Patties 32
Protein 9
Protein Powder
Banana & Peanut Milkshake 174
Brilliant Banana Shake 168
Chocolate & Berry Shake 167
Power Protein Shake 170
Vanilla Pancakes & Apricots 181
Yogurt Shake 175
Pumpkin
Powerful Pumpkin Mash 156
Pumpin' Pumpkin Pancakes 46
Pumpkin & Pine Nut Casserole 103
Pumpkin seeds
Mixed Seed Topper 151

Q

Quinoa
Beef Chili Con Carne 92
Carrot, Quinoa & Tarragon Soup 140
Chili Beef & Mango Salsa 81
Garlic Stuffed Mushrooms 101
Mexican Beans & Quinoa 95
Mighty Quinoa Breakfast Cereal 29
Mighty Stuffed Peppers 62
Pumpkin & Pine Nut Casserole 103
Rasin & root veg stew 106
Strong Spaghetti Squash Quinoa 99

R

Rutabaga
Parsnip & Rutabaga Chips 153

S

Salmon 114
Salmon Burgers With Avocado 122
Salmon Fillet & Pesto Mash 115
Sardines
Bulk-Up Sardines With Lemon, Garlic & Parsley 117

Scallops
  Scallops With Cauliflower & Chili
    129
  Seafood Kebabs & Cucumber
    Salad 138
Sea Bass
  Fennel & Olive Sea Bass 116
Shrimp
  Calamari & Shrimp Paella 114
  Coconut Shrimp & Noodles 130
  Garlic & Lemon Shrimp Linguine
    133
Sole
  Tomato & Walnut Sole 121
Spaghetti squash
  Spaghetti Squash & Yellow Lentil
    Soup 141
  Strong Spaghetti Squash Quinoa
    99
Spinach
  Spinach Pesto & Crudites 160
Swede
  Lemon Chicken With Swede &
    Kale Puree 66
  Powerful Pumpkin Mash 156
Sweet Potato
  Barbell Beef Curry 80
  Eggplant & Sweet Potato Lasa-
    gne 87
  Homemade Sweet Potato Fries
    154
  Langoustine & Sweet Potato
    Fries 120
  Raisin & Root Veg Stew 106
  Salmon Fillet & Pesto Mash 115
  Sweet Potato Cottage Pie 91
  Sweet Potato Pancakes 44
Swordfish
  Spicy Swordfish Steaks 131

T

Tangerine
  Tangerine Twist 169
Tempah
  Chinese Tempah Stir Fry 104
  Lime & Ginger Tempah 112
Tofu
  Chili & Honey Squash With Crispy
    Kale & Tofu 111
  Strawberry Mousse 177

Toasted Sesame & Peanut Tofu 97
Training Tofu Broth 94
Vegan Lasagne 96
Trout
  Rainbow Trout 119
  Smoked Trout Fish Cakes 128
Tuna
  Terrific Tuna Nicoise 125
  Tuna Steaks With Nutty Green
    Beans 135
Turkey
  Bodybuilding Fajitas 61
  Caribbean Turkey Thighs 63
  Mighty Mini Meatloaves 36
  Tasty Turkey Burgers 54
  Training Turkey Kebabs 57
  Turkey Bacon Omelette 39
  Turkey & Cranberry Sauce 68
  Turkey Meatballs & Couscous 70
  Turkey & Tabbouleh Salad 159

W

Water 12
Wholemeal oats
  Banana & Hazelnut Oatmeal 40
  Bounty Oats 30
  Brilliant Breakfast Bircher 35
  Brilliant Buckwheat Breakfast 31
  Cherry Protein Porridge 48
  Pecan & Dark Chocolate Chip Cook-
    ies 178
  Perfect Pancakes 41
  Power Protein Shake 170
  Scallion & Goats Cheese Pancakes
    110
  Sweet Potato Pancakes 44
  Workout Waffles 42

Z

Zucchini
  Cheeky Chicken Curry 65
  Spanish Paella 107
  White Bean & Med Veg Soup 146
  Zesty Zucchini Pasta & Protein
    Peas 109
  Zucchini, Bulghar Wheat And Egg-
    plant Salad 163